Advance Praise for *A Tale of Two Governments*

"A most timely book helping the American church to remember how 'two kingdoms' theology shaped the Western legal tradition to the service of both church and state."

Carl Esbeck
Professor of Law
University of Missouri

"In this fine, succinct work, the authors lead readers through a maze with simplicity and clarity. What we now have is a work that reviews the biblical, historical, and legal propriety of biblical church discipline. Every church needs this in its library; and every church staff owes it to its flock to read and acquaint itself with this fine work."

David W. Hall
Pastor, Midway Presbyterian Church
Author, *Calvin in the Public Square*

"In *A Tale of Two Governments*, Robert Renaud and Lael Weinberger have done a superb job of describing the jurisdictional separation of the authority of church and state governments—historically, legally, and Biblically. *A Tale of Two Governments* is an invaluable resource to a proper understanding of religious freedom and religious liberty in our Country. I encourage everyone to take time to read this outstanding work."

Roy S. Moore
President, Foundation for Moral Law
Former Chief Justice, Alabama Supreme Court

"In their book, *A Tale of Two Governments*, Robert J. Renaud and Lael D. Weinberger make the legal and biblical case for church discipline. Thank God! This book is an important contribution."

Rick Scarborough
Vision America

"As a professor who teaches both biblical dispute resolution and church/state relations, I recommend this book for students, pastors, attorneys and others who study church/state issues. As a practicing mediator working with churches in conflict, I am pleased there is finally a scholarly work that makes an historical argument for the necessity of modern day use of church discipline as a process of restoration. Every seminary student and pastor should read this book."

Bryan H. Sanders
Professor of Government and Legal Studies
Evangel University

"Wise church leadership requires a familiarity with the relevant legal issues in order to minimize exposure to legal liability as the church pursues obedience to Christ and faithfulness to Scripture. Most of this requisite knowledge of the law, however, is most easily discoverable by those in the legal profession. But in this book, Renaud and Weinberger make that information available to leaders of local churches in an understandable way and in the context of Scripture and church history."

Donald S. Whitney
Associate Professor of Biblical Spirituality and Senior
Associate Dean for the School of Theology
Southern Baptist Theological Seminary

"Robert Renaud and Lael Weinberger's book is timely and well researched. It is so important for us to understand the historic understanding of church government and discipline, and the relationship between civil government and church government. Would that all pastors and denominational leaders would read this book."

Daniel Juster
Director, Tikkun Ministries, Jerusalem
Author, *Due Process: A Plea for Biblical Justice Among God's People*

"*A Tale of Two Governments* is superb. It will be a very useful resource. I know nothing else like it."

Thomas Ascol
Pastor, Grace Baptist Church
Executive Director, Founders Ministries

"How can my church exercise discipline without offending the Constitution and the law? To exercise discipline safely and soundly, the Church needs the guidance of a Bible scholar, an expert on church history and theology, and a jurist who knows the Constitution, the case law, and the statutes that affect church discipline. Robert Renaud and Lael Weinberger fill all of these roles admirably in *A Tale of Two Governments*. No pastor or church officer should enter the minefield of church discipline without reading this book."

John A. Eidsmoe
Professor of Law, Oak Brook College of Law
Legal counsel, Foundation for Moral Law
Author of *Christianity and the Constitution*

"This book should be added to every Christian's library as there is really nothing like it available today. With historical and legal precision, Renaud and Weinberger have raised the issues that every church member ought to understand. The biblical and historical record is clear: there is a jurisdictional principle that establishes the complementary but separate roles of the church and the state."

Scott T. Brown
Pastor, Hope Baptist Church

"Read this book if you care about protecting the purity of the church from the wiles of the Enemy, and from the wiles of the courtroom. A meticulously researched and articulately crafted book that every pastor, church officer, and Christian leader must read."

Douglas Bond
Author of *The Betrayal*
Ruling elder, Presbyterian Church in America

"In *A Tale of Two Governments*, Robert Renaud and Lael Weinberger provide us with a remarkable vision for how to recover Biblical faithfulness in our churches. In addition though, they also show us the way toward a substantial reformation of our entire culture—if only the church would actually be the church."

George Grant
Pastor, Parish Presbyterian Church

A TALE OF TWO GOVERNMENTS

CHURCH DISCIPLINE, THE COURTS, AND THE SEPARATION OF CHURCH AND STATE

By Robert J. Renaud & Lael D. Weinberger

DUNROBIN
PUBLISHING

www.dunrobin.us

For permission to reproduce contact:
Dunrobin Publishing
www.dunrobin.us
permissions@dunrobin.us

ISBN 978-0-9832363-8-2

To our parents:

Bill and Carole Renaud
and
David and Betty Weinberger

TABLE OF CONTENTS

FOREWORD BY JOHN MACARTHUR

Perhaps no aspect of church life is more misunderstood, neglected, and abused than church discipline. Christ's own instructions regarding this issue are found in Matthew 18:15-20. He said sin in the fellowship of God's people must be confronted—privately at first, but then publicly if necessary. Sinning church members who repent at any point in the process can be restored to a holy walk, fully and freely forgiven. But if the person remains unrepentant when every avenue of appeal is exhausted, he or she must be excommunicated.

Of course, putting people out of the church is never the desired outcome of church discipline; restoration is. In each step of the process the *immediate* goal is to bring the disobedient Christian back to repentance, back into full fellowship—back under the blessings of God's forgiveness. But the purity of the church is the *ultimate* and non-negotiable goal, so excommunication does become necessary at times when people persist in sin despite persistent pleas for their repentance.

How important is it for the church to discipline sinning members? *It is absolutely essential to the health and vitality of the church.* This is not an optional or negotiable issue. Sin is like leaven—it spreads, and it will infect the whole body if not purged (1 Corinthians 5:1-13). A congregation where known, unrepentant sin is openly tolerated is a spiritually dangerous place, not a safe fold for the flock of God. No wonder the Reformers and their spiritual heirs have always listed the faithful practice of church discipline as one of the essential marks of a true church.

Over the past century or so, however, evangelical churches have been growing lax about the practice of church discipline. With the rise of pragmatic, seeker-sensitive, attractional philosophies of ministry, some evangelical leaders have even repudiated the duty of discipline completely. Public relations concerns have taken precedence over purity. The idea of openly confronting sin simply does not meet the test of consumer demand. Besides, church discipline tends to make unbelievers uncomfortable, and that goes against the counsel of virtually every leading church-growth expert.

How different that is from the biblical pattern! When Ananias and Sapphira sinned, they provoked God's immediate displeasure and fell dead on the spot. It was a vivid reminder that death is sin's wage (Romans 6:23); those who live according to the flesh will die (8:13); and it is a fearful thing to fall into the hands of the living God (Hebrews 10:31). Scripture says in the wake of the Ananias-Sapphira incident, "Great fear came upon the whole church and upon all who heard of these things" (Acts 5:11).

In God's mercy, most sins don't incur such severe and immediate retribution directly from God's hand. Instead, the discipline process is a prolonged, gracious summons to repentance. The steps of discipline are deliberately designed so that the response to the original discovery of sin is as discreet as possible, but if the sinning member refuses to heed the plea, then a widening circle of church members must become involved. This signifies the importance and the urgency of the need to turn from sin.

The process Jesus outlined has four basic steps. *Step one* is as private as possible: "If your brother sins against you, go and tell him his fault, between you and him alone. If he listens to you, you have gained your brother" (Matthew 18:15).

But if the sinning person refuses to repent, the matter cannot stay private. *Step two* therefore broadens the circle ever so slightly: "If he does not listen, take one or two others along with you, that every charge may be established by the evidence of two or three witnesses" (v. 16).

If there still is no repentance, *step three* entails informing the whole church so that everyone in the fellowship may pursue the sinning member and seek his or her repentance: "If he refuses to listen to [the two or three witnesses], tell it to the church" (v. 17).

If at that point the person still refuses to repent, *step four*—excommunication—becomes necessary. Even that step, drastic as it seems, actually represents the gracious postponement of sin's full wages while providing an extended opportunity for repentance and restoration (cf. Hebrews 3:13-15). I have seen people turn from their sin and seek the Lord's forgiveness even after reaching that fourth step in the discipline process. Humanly speaking, there is always that hope, because when all the stages of discipline have been faithfully followed (with the whole church being informed as instructed), the result should be the same as when Ananias and Sapphira died—a healthy fear of God and a holy loathing for sin comes upon the whole church and all who hear.

None of that is politically correct today, of course. In secular culture, the dominant belief is that nothing done in private by consenting adults can legitimately be regarded as sinful. Even among professing Christians, many think sin by definition is a private matter between God and the sinner—no one else's business. Meanwhile, the entertainment and news media have been on a decades-long campaign to whitewash the most abominable kinds of sin. Courts and politicians have been chipping away at moral values on the one hand and religious freedom on the other, finding "constitutional rights" for activities long deemed abominable while imposing more restrictions and regulations than ever on churches.

In such a culture, it should come as no surprise that church discipline is seen as draconian, unenlightened, archaic—particularly the ideas of exposing sin and excommunicating unrepentant sinners. The bottom line is that church discipline done as Christ commanded contradicts the postmodern notions of moral freedom, tolerance, diversity, and the inviolability of personal preferences. For several generations, western culture has also fostered a deep suspicion of authority, an unbreakable addiction to self-esteem, and an irrational aversion to reproof, rebuke, correction—or anything that might make someone feel "marginalized."

When biblical values contrast that starkly with a culture's values, anyone seeking to live in accord with biblical standards will suffer persecution (2 Timothy 3:12). In these litigious times, the courts have often been the place where faithful churches have been put to the test. Lawsuits filed against churches for doing their biblical duty have become almost commonplace. The more such lawsuits make headlines, the more new lawsuits are filed.

At the opposite end of the spectrum, there is no shortage of abusive cults, dictatorial religious leaders, and professional clergymen (including some unqualified men in positions of leadership in evangelical churches) who misapply the principles of discipline, desecrate its true purpose, and use it as a truncheon to pummel people rather than an instrument of rescue and cleansing for lambs who have wandered and fallen into sin. I occasionally encounter religious leaders with a Pharisaical bent who like to wield the threat of excommunication like an ox-goad. Some of them claim prophetic authority that even the apostles never resorted to (cf. 2 Corinthians 12:12-21). For them, excommunication is not merely a last resort in cases of serious, unrepentant sin, but an easy means of extorting agreement from anyone who has dared to question them.

Jesus' teaching about church discipline consumes very little space in the New Testament. Everything He said on the subject is condensed into just three verses in Matthew 18. But the application of those principles has never been simple, and especially not in a culture such as ours. Still, it is our duty to deal with sin in the manner Christ prescribed. We must do it in the spirit of Galatians 6:1: "In a spirit of gentleness. Keep watch on yourself, lest you too be tempted." We also need to be aware of the legal pitfalls. And we always need to keep at the forefront of our hearts and minds what is the true goal and purpose of the discipline process: rescuing souls from the destructive effects of sin (cf. Matthew 18:12-14).

I'm glad more and more evangelicals are beginning to recognize the wisdom and biblical necessity of Jesus' plan for church discipline. When I began in full-time ministry more than four decades ago, I did not know of a single evangelical church where the Matthew 18 process was followed consistently. Christians in circles where I ministered were not well-taught in the matter of how to confront or minister to fellow Christians who have fallen into sin. That has changed over the years, thankfully. Today there are several fine books that discuss church discipline from a biblical and exegetical perspective.

But this book in particular stands in a gap that I've long hoped to see occupied. Robert Renaud and Lael Weinberger deal with the legal and constitutional questions currently being raised as cases of church discipline are increasingly subjected to review by secular courts.

Is it possible to apply the vital principle of church discipline, render to Caesar what is Caesar's, and still steer clear of the most serious legal dangers in a litigious age such as ours? Yes, it is. Renaud and Weinberger chart a clear road-map through the major land-mines that surround this question. The book is instructive not only as it looks at church discipline from a biblical point of view, but also in its crystal-clear analysis of the legal pitfalls, its discussion of the constitutional issues regarding church and state, and the practical advice it gives.

May you and every other reader of this book be encouraged and emboldened in obedience to Christ, and may we apply ourselves to the purity and health of our local church bodies, for the honor and glory of our Master.

John MacArthur
Pastor
Grace Community Church
Sun Valley, California

INTRODUCTION

In 2007, the Texas Supreme Court heard a case that brought together half a dozen controversial issues. A pastor. Marriage counseling. Church discipline. The separation of church and state. The limits of government power.

In 2007, we (Bob and Lael) were in the middle of law school. We had been friends for a number of years, a friendship that began around a shared set of interests. We were history buffs. We loved to discuss and debate legal issues. We were committed Christians. We collected books on theology and church history. We were passionate about the importance of the church.

So when we saw the Texas Supreme Court case—*Westbrook v. Penley*—we were instantly intrigued. It seemed designed to bring together all of our interests.

* * *

The case started innocuously enough. Before becoming pastor of Crossland Community Bible Church outside of Dallas, C.L. "Buddy" Westbrook was a licensed professional marriage counselor. After becoming a pastor, he continued to use this training when advising members of his congregation. His past experience and his current job seemed to fit together nicely—at least until he was sued.[1]

In his former job as a full-time marriage counselor, Buddy had given several counseling sessions to Peggy Penley and her husband, Benjamin. When Buddy became the pastor of Crossland, Penley and her husband joined Crossland Church. But her marriage did not improve, and it was only a matter of months before she separated from her husband. Penley and her husband began attending group marriage-counseling sessions.

It soon became evident that there was no saving the marriage. In a private counseling session, Penley took Buddy aside and told him that she was involved in an affair with another man and she was going to get a divorce. Buddy informed her that her conduct was contrary to Scripture. He urged her to get out of her illicit relationship and repent before God. Penley was unmoved.

Pastor Westbrook knew that, according to the Bible, it's always preferable to get the issue resolved privately if possible. But if a Christian is in sin, and remains unrepentant after being confronted, then it becomes necessary to get some more help. Buddy informed the other church elders of the situation with Penley, and they collectively approached her about it. She was again unrepentant.

As a final step, Pastor Westbrook informed the church. He wrote a letter to the church members that described the biblical procedure of church discipline from Matthew 18. The procedure starts by a private meeting with the "brother or sister in sin," urging repentance and, if that was unsuccessful, then bringing two or three others to encourage the "brother or sister in sin" to repent.

> If the one in sin "refuses to listen" to this group of two
> or three, then the instructions are to "tell it to the church."
> If the one in sin now "listens," the process is complete—
> and we have "won our brother or sister."

Notice, however, "if he refuses to listen even to the
church, let him be to you as a Gentile and a tax-gatherer."
[Matthew 18:17] As somewhat of an oversimplification,
this means to treat the one in sin as an outsider. Through
their continuing sin, they forfeit their membership in the
church, and the members of the church are to break fellowship with them.

The letter explained that Penley intended to divorce her husband
without biblical justification. It said that she was involved in a "biblically
inappropriate" relationship with another man and that she remained
unrepentant after repeated admonitions. It was now the time for church
members to "break fellowship" with Penley with the goal of bringing
about repentance and restoration. The letter concluded with a reminder
that this was a "members-only issue, not to be shared with those outside
[the congregation]."

Church discipline is never easy. But the real difficulties for the pastor
and the church were still to come. Peggy Penley filed a lawsuit against
Buddy Westbrook and Crossland Church, alleging that Westbrook violated his professional duties as a counselor by disclosing the information
to the church elders and members.

* * *

When we read this case, we recognized that there was a lot more at
stake than just whether a Texas pastor wins or loses a lawsuit. The bigger
issue was whether the courts could tell churches how to run their affairs.
Could a court tell a church that the pastor can't talk to the other elders?
Could a court tell a church who can and can't be a member?

What was really at stake was the meaning of religious freedom.

3

What was at stake was the meaning of the separation of church and state.

Many Christians are afraid of "separation of church and state" because the phrase is so often used in a way that is hostile to religion. A lot of people today think that the separation of church and state means that God and faith and religion can't be mentioned in public. But this distorts the original meaning of separation of church and state.

Even as law students, we knew enough history to know that "separation of church and state" was originally a Christian idea. It was developed and taught by pastors and theologians for centuries. It was a principle that protected the church from being taken over by the state.

When we saw the decision by the Texas Supreme Court in the *Westbrook* case, we were thrilled. The court nailed all the issues (we'll look at it in more detail in chapter 6). The court's opinion almost seemed to say, "The original meaning of the separation of church and state still survives." And that's good news for pastors. It's good news for churches. It's good news for Christians. It's good news for every American who cares about liberty.

We decided that we should write an article about the *Westbrook* case and the forgotten history that it brought back to life. Somehow, we managed to find time away from our studies to research and write a law review article. To our delight, we soon had a publisher. Our article appeared in the *Northern Kentucky Law Review* some months later.[2]

We shared copies of our article with a lot of our friends, especially lawyers and pastors. We were yet more delighted to find that so many of the people we shared it with appreciated it. But law review articles are academic articles aimed at lawyers and law professors. Several of the people who read our article began to encourage us to write something else on this subject, something that could be read by a wider audience than just lawyers. Pastors needed to know how to avoid lawsuits. Christians needed to know what the "separation of church and state" originally meant. Americans needed to know what this means for a free

4

society. That's when we started to work on this book.

As we researched and wrote over the last five years, we were continually amazed at how much material we could include. The more we learned about the history, the richer the story became. The story also became increasingly timely, as the issues we were writing about kept appearing in the news.

Church discipline was regularly getting media attention. One news item bordered on the humorous. "A divorced Jacksonville woman said her former church has threatened to 'go public with her sins,'" the news article began. It went on to quote the woman: "Because I have a boyfriend that I'm involved with . . . to not be married to that person is a sin. . . . On January 4, my sins will be told to the church, publicly, with my children sitting in the church and my friends."[3]

It certainly was ironic that the woman had no problem talking about the matter to local and national news reporters who then broadcast the news about her "sins" and her dispute with the church on television and the internet.[4] The article named the woman and displayed her picture. After this kind of "going public," we wondered why this woman didn't think it would be better to just go through the church proceeding and be done with it.

In January 2008, the *Wall Street Journal* ran a feature article on the "comeback" of church discipline.[5] This "comeback" has precipitated a spate of lawsuits; more than two dozen have been filed related to church discipline in the past decade, the article reported.[6]

Some fifty years ago, almost no one would have thought of suing their pastor if they were excluded from communion or were offended by his way of counseling. How then did the recent spate of lawsuits come about?

1980 was a turning point for the way Americans thought of churches and the law, according to legal historian Mark Weitz.[7] It was in 1980 that a highly publicized lawsuit began against a large church in southern

California. The figure behind the lawsuit was Walter Nally, a heartbroken father whose son had committed suicide. Nally had become convinced that fault for the suicide lay with the church where his son had received counseling. Nally sued the church and its pastor, the well-known author, educator, and broadcaster John MacArthur. Nally's legal theory was "clergy malpractice." After nine years of litigation, he lost the case at the California Supreme Court.[8]

The message of *Nally v. Grace Community Church* could have been that suing churches is a good way to get in the news but a bad way to make money. But more fundamentally, *Nally* began an era in which lawsuits against churches became increasingly common. Fortunately, abnormal tragedies like suicide are not the normal context for these lawsuits. Unfortunately, normal disciplinary actions—church discipline—are. Church discipline is not just the stuff of local churches, presbyteries, and synods any more.

As we continued working on this book in the years after law school, we kept finding more news stories about church discipline and more court cases involving churches and pastors. The issue wasn't going to go away.

As if to make this point even stronger, the U.S. Supreme Court agreed to hear a church case just as we were finishing a first draft of our book in 2011. For the first time in decades, the U.S. Supreme Court was going to decide a case involving the authority of courts to intervene in internal church matters. It was the very issue we were writing about (and our original journal article was even discussed in one of the amicus briefs).

When the Supreme Court issued its decision in January 2012, we were—again—thrilled. The Court got the central issue right. It recognized that the proper relationship of the church and the state was on the line. And it protected the historical, original meaning of that separation. It was good news for pastors, Christians, and all Americans.

What is that good news? It's the good news that the government is limited and not all-powerful—and that the church in America has the freedom and the legal protection that Christians have struggled to obtain for centuries. To understand this, we'll have to take a historical journey. Indeed, looking at the story of church-state relations over two millennia, it is striking that the seemingly new debates over the authority of the church to govern itself (by exercising church discipline) are not new at all. They're as old as western culture itself. For centuries, the authority of the church to govern itself was a flashpoint of controversy.

Many of the lessons learned through these centuries of struggle, trial and error, reformations and revolutions are embodied in the American legal system to this day. Sadly, few Americans know about them. But we need to know. Church leaders need to know in order to find practical solutions for churches threatened by litigation. Christians need to know in order to understand the place of the church in the culture. And we all need to know, as citizens, if we are to understand the relationship between church and state.

PART I: TWO THOUSAND YEARS OF CHURCH AND STATE

CHAPTER 1. THE THEOLOGY OF CHURCH AND STATE

"You may deem it a strange prophecy, but I predict that the time will come in this once free America when the battle for religious liberty will have to be fought over again, and will probably be lost, because the people are already ignorant of its true basis and conditions."[9] A theologian named Robert Dabney wrote these words in 1897. In retrospect, his comment appears prescient. Religious liberty issues are constantly in the news today. Over the last few decades, there has been a seemingly endless string of legal battles over prayer in public places, displays of the Ten Commandments, legislative and military chaplains, and Bible studies in government buildings, to name a few of the issues that have come up. They all generate discussion about the relationship between religion and government, religious liberty and government establishment, church and state. But the historical foundations of religious liberty and the separation of church and state are largely forgotten. Today, there are few phrases in public policy parlance more misinterpreted, misquoted, and misapplied than the "separation of church and state."

When American Christians hear the phrase "separation of church and state," what do they normally think of? Many think of the court cases prohibiting public displays of the Ten Commandments or ending school prayer. In recent years, Michael Newdow's many high-profile lawsuits to stop public religious expressions have grabbed headlines. His most famous lawsuit was an attempt to remove the reference to God from the Pledge of Allegiance.[10] Then he made the news with lawsuits to keep references to God out of the presidential inauguration.[11] Traditionally, presidents have added the words "So help me God," to their oath of office and ministers begin the inauguration with prayer.[12] In 2009, Newdow tried to get an injunction that would bar both the prayer and the reference to God in the oath from the inauguration ceremony—not just for that year, but for all future inaugurations.[13] He wasn't successful in court. But Newdow (and other secular activists like him) have been very successful at claiming the phrase "separation of church and state" as their own.

So, in the minds of many, "separation of church and state" is the rallying cry of the most dogmatic advocates of separation between religion and the public square. Some legal scholars have called this position "strict separationism."[14] And strict separationism *is* a problem. It is quite understandable that many Christians who care about the public square have developed an almost allergic negative reaction to the phrase, "separation of church and state."[15]

But the allergic reaction has itself become a problem. Too often, we see Christians reacting against the phrase but missing the larger issue. If someone mentions the phrase, "separation of church and state," an all-too-common reaction from a concerned Christian is the retort, "That phrase isn't in the Constitution." Technically true, it isn't. But the principle of church-state separation *is* implicitly embodied in its First Amendment. The church and the state are kept separate by not allowing the federal government to establish a national church as well as by recognizing the people's freedom to worship according to the dictates of their own consciences.

Separation of church and state, at its most basic, simply means that the church and the state are separate and distinct institutions. Confusion arises when the word "church" gets equated with religion in its broadest sense. Then we end up with the separation of God from the public square or the separation of God from the realm of civil government. That might be what some secularist activists want, but it's not the original meaning of the separation of church and state. The separation of church and state, as we shall see, is an important, healthy, and indeed biblical doctrine. It was developed, in large part, by Christian theologians.[16] Even the term, "separation of church and state," was used by theologians before it was used by politicians.[17] It's time that we as Christians begin to appreciate it.

TWO GOVERNMENTS UNDER GOD

In one of the most famous lines in the New Testament, Jesus Christ answered one of the most important legal and jurisdictional questions of the ages: What authority may be rightfully exercised by a civil magistrate?[18] His simple proposition was this: "Render therefore unto Caesar the things which be Caesar's and unto God the things which be God's" (Matthew 22:21).[19]

The theologians of the Reformation recognized two sides to Jesus' answer. Both sides are essential for a proper theology of church and state. First, Christ recognizes that the civil government does have legitimate authority by His command to "render to Caesar the things that are Caesar's."[20] John Calvin explained the necessity of civil jurisdiction in these terms: "[T]he amount of it therefore is, that those who destroy political order are rebellious against God, and therefore, that obedience to princes and magistrates is always joined to the worship and fear of God . . . ."[21]

Second, Christ denies that the civil ruler has an absolute power over citizens. Notwithstanding the obligation to Caesar, we must render "to God the things that are God's."[22] As Psalm 24:1 declares, "The earth is the LORD's, and the fullness thereof; the world, and they that dwell therein." Clearly, then, Caesar cannot be lord over all.[23] Only Christ can make that claim. As Calvin wrote, "[I]f princes claim any part of the authority of God, we ought not to obey them any farther than can be done without offending God."[24]

As the Reformers saw it, the two sides of the coin merge into one overriding principle: Civil government has its proper sphere of authority under the ultimate authority of God. The eighteenth century pastor and Bible commentator, John Gill, explained: "[S]ubjection to civil magistrates is not inconsistent with the reverence and fear of God; all are to have their dues rendered unto them, without intrenching [*sic*] upon one another."[25]

Yet civil government is not the only God-ordained government. The church is another distinct governmental sphere. Jesus Christ is the head of the church, Paul wrote in Colossians 1:18. Calvin noted that Paul "speaks chiefly of government. He shews . . . that it is Christ that alone has authority to govern the church."[26]

From these principles, the Reformers recognized the church and the state as two forms of government. Both were administered by men, but both were ordained by God and under His ultimate authority. Both were created with different spheres of authority. In Romans 13:4, the "sword" represents the civil government's power. The church does not have the power of the sword, but it does have the power of church discipline. The reformers called this the power of the "keys," after Christ's reference in Matthew 16:19 to the "keys of the kingdom."[27] Neither had sovereignty over the other, and both were equally ultimate in their own spheres.

THE HEBREW MODEL

This framework that the New Testament establishes—that church and state are two different, coexisting, and equally ultimate governments under God—was recognized and embraced by the Bible expositors of the Reformation. They recognized also that the institutional separation of church and state was modeled in the Old Testament, long before Christ's earthly advent.[28] In the book of Exodus, the position of civil magistrate and priest are established separately.[29] These offices remained separate even after the Babylonian captivity, with its otherwise significant alterations in the social structure.[30] Furthermore, in two key narrative passages, the institutional separation of church and state are presented as divinely ordained. In both of these narratives, serious consequences followed when established jurisdictional boundaries were violated.

In the first passage, Saul, king of Israel, was worried by the absence of Samuel the prophet on the eve of a battle.[31] To encourage his men, he proceeded to offer the sacrifice to God that only Samuel was authorized to discharge. Upon arriving on the scene, Samuel rebuked Saul, "You have done foolishly. You have not kept the command of the LORD your God, with which he commanded you. For then the LORD would have established your kingdom over Israel forever. But now your kingdom shall not continue." (1 Samuel 13:13–14 ESV.)

In the second passage, Uzziah king of Judah entered the temple in Jerusalem to burn incense to the Lord,[32] thus usurping the responsibilities of the priests.[33] The priests confronted him for this breach of jurisdictional boundaries:

> [T]hey withstood King Uzziah and said to him, "It is
> not for you, Uzziah, to burn incense to the LORD, but for
> the priests, the sons of Aaron, who are consecrated to
> burn incense. Go out of the sanctuary, for you have done
> wrong, and it will bring you no honor from the LORD
> God."[34]

The consequence of Uzziah overstepping his jurisdictional place was serious. The scriptural account states that, immediately after the priests' rebuke, God struck Uzziah with leprosy.

Both of these passages present the highest civil authority, the king, taking upon himself the administration of a "church" function. In both cases, the errant king was severely reprimanded and received divine judgment. The lesson was clear: the theoretical principle of distinct jurisdictions had practical consequences. The jurisdictional boundaries could not be violated but at the risk of God's judgment.

In addition to these negative examples, a third narrative passage presents a positive example of the scriptural doctrine of the separation of church and state. Jehoshaphat, a righteous king of Judah,[35] implemented a jurisdictional distinction between ecclesiastical and civil governments as he appointed officers in his administration: "Amariah the chief priest is over you in all matters of the LORD; and Zebadiah the son of Ishmael, the ruler of the house of Judah, for all the king's matters . . ." (2 Chronicles 19:11). This is an excellent example of godly leadership recognizing and respecting the different jurisdictions of what we would now call "church" and state. In the words of John Gill, we see the "high priest, presid[ing] in [the] court of all things sacred," and "the prince of the tribe of Judah" handling matters "related to civil government."[36]

JURISDICTION AND SPHERE SOVEREIGNTY

The concept of church and state as separate institutions results in a division of jurisdiction. The word "jurisdiction" is a combination of two Latin roots, *juris*, law, and *dictio*, speaking. Jurisdiction is literally the power to speak law to a particular situation.[37] A division of jurisdiction means that no one source of law can speak to everything. There are limits to what the government can speak to (the king can't offer sacrifices in the temple), and to what the church can speak to (the church can't bring murderers to trial and execute them). The basic question of jurisdictions is not, *what should we do?*, but rather, *who should do what?*

Suppose a civil government took murder off the books as a crime. Now the government was failing in fulfilling one of its basic biblical obligations: to "bear the sword" to punish evildoing.[38] Could a church step into the void as a last resort when other institutions fail? Suppose a church appoints a deacon as a constable to track down a murderer on the loose in the community. The church elders act as a jury and the pastor as a judge, and together they convict and sentence the murderer the deacon catches. Another deacon electrocutes the sentenced murderer in the church basement. Is this biblical? Hardly. Should someone have done something about the problem of a murderer roaming at large in the community? Certainly. But Scripture is very specific about who should have done something: the state. The church has no authority to take up the "power of the sword." Jurisdictional spheres are important, because what is a good, wise, even righteous act in one jurisdiction may be bad, unwise, and unrighteous when done by another jurisdiction.

The concept of jurisdictional boundaries is encapsulated in the theological idea of "sphere sovereignty": different spheres of life have their own self-contained authority. The church and the state are each sovereign (under God) within their own spheres. The phrase, "sphere sovereignty" (in Dutch, *souvereiniteit in eigen sfeer*) comes from the Netherlands. Drawing on a long history of Reformed theological thinking about church-state issues, Groen van Prinsterer introduced this expression in 1862 to explain exactly what we have been considering in this chapter—that church and state are independent of each other, even though both are subject to God's commandments.[39]

The greatest explanation of sphere sovereignty was provided by the Dutch polymath Abraham Kuyper.[40] Kuyper was a man with wide-ranging experience in many different "spheres" of life: pastor, theologian, journalist, newspaper editor, founder of the Free University of Amsterdam, and prime minister of the Netherlands from 1901 to 1905.[41] (Someone once said that for Americans to understand Kuyper, they have to imagine a theologian who founds Princeton University, edits the *New York Times*, and becomes president of the United States.)

Kuyper came to the United States in 1898 to give a prestigious lecture series at Princeton, and it was in those lectures that he brought the terminology of "sphere sovereignty" to America.[42] He explained that there are many different areas of life (Kuyper would know); church and state are some of the most basic "spheres." Each has some authority to act within their respective spheres. None has unlimited authority.[43] Each answers to God for its conduct.

In defining the phrase "sphere sovereignty," sovereignty is used in a limited sense. Absolute sovereignty can only rest in God, as Kuyper was careful to explain in his lectures at Princeton: "The dominating principle . . . [is] *the sovereignty of the Triune God over the whole Cosmos*, in all spheres and kingdoms, visible and invisible."[44]

Thus, no human institution is "sovereign" in the absolute sense. Because of this, no human institution has absolute power. God possesses all power and authority, and He delegates limited amounts to mankind: some to the church, some to the state, some to other spheres of authority such as the individual and the family.[45]

Kuyper specifically addressed the position of the church in relation to the civil government. Speaking of the history of the Calvinist tradition, Kuyper explained the distinctions between the jurisdictions of church and state:

> Hence it is that the Calvinists have always struggled so
> proudly and courageously for the liberty, that is to say for
> the sovereignty, of the Church, within her own sphere
> . . . . In Christ, they contended, the Church has her own
> King. Her position in the State is not assigned her by

the permission of the Government, but jure divino. She has her own organization. She possesses her own office-bearers. And in a similar way she has her own gifts to distinguish truth from the lie. It is therefore her privilege, and not that of the State, to determine her own character-istics as the true Church, and to proclaim her own confes-sion as the confession of the truth.[46]

SPHERE SOVEREIGNTY AND FREEDOM

Abraham Kuyper explained in his Princeton lecture that the church, the family,

and so forth are all social spheres, which do not owe their existence to the State, and which do not derive the law of their life from the superiority of the state, but obey a high authority within their own bosom; an authority which rules, by the grace of God, just as the sovereignty of the State does. . . . These different developments of social life *have nothing above themselves but God.* . . . As you feel at once, this is the deeply interesting question of our *civil liberties.*[47]

What Kuyper meant by referring to civil liberties is that this division of power within society as a whole is actually what makes freedom and free societies possible. "The sovereignty of the State and sovereignty of the Church exist side by side, and they mutually limit each other," Kuyper said.[48] Others have noted the same thing. Michael McConnell, a distin-guished legal scholar and for some years a federal judge, explained that when a state is forced to recognize that the church possesses legitimate and distinct authorities, totalitarianism is thwarted:

The separation of church from state is the most powerful

possible refutation of the notion that the political sphere is omnicompetent—that it has rightful authority over all of life. If the state does not have power over the church, it follows that the power of the state is limited. The extent of state power need not be left to the discretion of rulers.[49]

This means that the jurisdictional separation of church and state is not only important for protecting the state from meddling with the church, or vice versa. It is important as well to preserve the independence of the individual from the tyranny of totalitarianism. Churches and other religious groups serve as "autonomous moral and political forces, intermediate institutions, separate heads of sovereignty vital to preventing majoritarian tyranny."[50] Even those with very little concern for issues of church government should nonetheless be grateful for this—and careful to preserve this healthy plurality of powers.

The theological foundations we have just looked at allow us to understand just how it is that "separation of church and state" is grounded in Scripture itself. It should also help us to understand better why there have been theologians throughout church history who recognized, and indeed embraced, this concept.

CHAPTER 1 IN A NUTSHELL...

- The separation of church and state does *not* mean the separation of God from government or the separation of religion from public life.
- The separation of church and state *does* mean that the church and the state are distinct institutions.
- Both church and state are ordained by God, but both have different roles.
- These different roles lead to church and state having different jurisdictions (the authority to "speak law" to a particular situation).

CHAPTER 2: CHURCH AND STATE FROM AUGUSTINE TO THE REFORMATION

To understand the modern relationship between church and state, we must start our historical investigation more than a millennium before the American founding, with early church leaders like Augustine and Gelasius. As we move through the centuries, we will observe that power struggles between church and state occurred at various points in the Middle Ages—often, the fruits of theological misunderstandings and imbalances in church and state. Yet the basic principles would always make a comeback. One of the key "comeback" moments was the Protestant Reformation, which recovered a balance (in the theory, if not always in the practice) of church-state relations at a time when jurisdictional thinking was at a low ebb. We'll take a closer look at that when we get to it.

In our journey, we will be paying special attention to the people, documents, and events that contributed more or less directly to our American heritage. This means that as we move through history, our attention will be increasingly focused on what was happening in the British Isles. Our first stop, though, is far removed from England.

THE FIRST 500 YEARS

Northern Africa in the fourth century was a prosperous Roman dominion. For many years, the North Africans had lived life without concerning themselves about what was going on in the rest of the empire. Even as the Roman Empire was crumbling around it, the Algerian region provided a relatively safe harbor for refugees from Rome itself. It was in the Algerian city of Hippo that a churchman began to address many of the questions that people were asking as they watched the empire crumble from afar.[51]

This churchman, Augustine of Hippo, now occupies a seminal position in church history as one of the most influential theologians of his generation—or of any generation. He began writing his magnum opus, *The City of God*, to answer the questions of his own society, a society in a state of flux. But *The City of God* had a life much longer, and an impact much broader, than merely addressing one society in one time and place. Augustine's work cast a large scale vision for the Christian in society. Augustine did not directly address the relationship of the church to the state. Augustine talked about two distinct "cities," the city of God and the city of man.

> The city of God consisted of all those who were predes-
> tined to salvation, bound by the love of God, and devoted
> to a life of Christian piety, morality, and worship led by
> the Christian clergy. The city of man consisted of all the
> things of this sinful world, and the political and social
> institutions that God had created to maintain a modicum
> of order and peace.[52]

These concepts did not translate directly into a distinction between church and state, but it wasn't hard for people to think in these terms once Augustine's powerful metaphor took hold on the imagination. As the historian John Witte has written, "It was crucial . . . that the spiritual and temporal powers that prevailed in these two cities remain separate in function. Even though Christianity became the one established religion of the Roman Empire, patronized and protected by the Roman state authorities, Augustine and other Church Fathers insisted that state power remain separate from church power."[53]

Some sixty years after Augustine,[54] in the late 5th century, Pope Gelasius I developed the idea of "two kingdoms" into an explicit political formula.[55] Writing to Anastasius I, the emperor reigning in Constantinople, Gelasius stated,

> Two there are, august emperor, by which this world is
> chiefly ruled, the sacred authority of the priesthood and
> the royal power .... If the bishops themselves, recogniz-
> ing that the imperial office was conferred on you by divine
> disposition, obey your laws so far as the sphere of public
> order is concerned ... with what zeal, I ask you, ought you
> to obey those who have been charged with administering
> the sacred mysteries [in matters of religion]?[56]

This letter clearly articulated the idea of church and state as jurisdictionally distinct spheres of authority.

The Gelasian theory served to uphold the independence of the church from state dominance in the tempestuous Byzantine era. Under Constantine, the Roman Empire had relocated its seat of government to the city that bore his name, Constantinople in Asia Minor (now known as Istanbul in modern day Turkey). That was in 330 AD, but as the centuries progressed, the western half of the empire weakened and then collapsed. Tensions grew between the eastern and western churches during this same time, and they eventually split into Roman Catholic and Eastern Orthodox camps. The traumatic repercussions of these splits reverberated through the palaces and churches of east and west. The Gelasian formula of church and state kept the balance in theory, with both a church and a state that coexisted in their own spheres of sovereignty. But this was in theory only. The practical reality was that, all too often, the actual balance of power depended on the relative powers of the "prelates" and the emperors. In other words, regardless of the theory, the stronger party (church or state) at any given time tried hard to assert supremacy over the other.[57]

CHANGE OF COURSE

In the eleventh century, the pressures of dealing with the Byzantine emperors was subsiding, and the Roman Catholic Church was becoming comfortable in its western sphere of influence. It was at this point that the church under Pope Gregory VII clearly abandoned the doctrine of distinct spheres of authority for church and state. Gregory VII powerfully asserted the power of the church. (Incidentally, the Reformers particularly disliked Gregory VII; Calvin called him "an impure and wicked man."[58]) The doctrine of distinct but coeval powers metamorphosed in his hands into a claim of papal supremacy: the church, and specifically the pope, above the state.[59]

The new relationship was graphically illustrated when the Holy Roman Emperor, Henry IV, clashed with Pope Gregory VII. It was common at the time for the kings to appoint bishops and other church officers as an exercise of royal authority.[60] Gregory set out to stop this practice and issued the *Dictatus Papae*, prohibiting laymen (including kings) from making appointments to church offices. Henry ignored the pope's edict, and when he set up a new bishop in Milan, Gregory warned him to desist or risk being deposed. Henry called the pope's bluff, only to discover that he was serious. Gregory excommunicated Henry in February 1076. Lest they too fall subject to judgment by the papal authority, the electors delivered Henry an ultimatum: obtain absolution from Gregory within a year and a day of the excommunication, or a new emperor will be chosen. Henry buckled under the pressure. Henry undertook an arduous winter journey to see the pope, then at the castle of Canossa, where he arrived in January of 1077. In a scene that became legendary, the penitent emperor waited at the pope's gate for three days, barefoot in the snow, before obtaining mercy and absolution from the pope. Gregory had dramatically established the supremacy of the church over the state.[61]

The medieval popes mostly followed the lead of Gregory. The Reformer Martin Bucer was to later comment on this episode in his 1538 work on church discipline, viewing it as a significant turning point in the rise of papal power:

> Once this pope had succeeded in bringing such an able, valiant and mighty emperor to the point where he had to throw himself on his mercy, the other popes followed the example of this pope and in this way increased their outward powers . . . ever more, until they were able to set themselves up as lords over the whole world, having all kingdoms and powers at their disposal and pleasure as their own property . . . with complete authority, which no-one on earth is to question.[62]

From the fifth through the eleventh centuries, the emperors had been called the "vicar of Christ," and the popes were only called the "vicar of Saint Peter."[63] Now, to reinforce the claim of papal supremacy, Innocent III added the emperor's title to his own: "Vicarius Dei," the "vicar of God."[64] Pope Boniface VIII acknowledged that there were "two swords, namely, the spiritual and the temporal,"[65] but these swords were not representing two coeval powers of church and state. Instead, as one scholar has explained, both of the swords "were in the power of the church, the former being wielded 'by the church [ab ecclesia]' and the latter by the government but 'on behalf of the church [pro ecclesia].'"[66]

The Reformation occurred during the time when papal supremacy claims reigned dominant. Because the Reformation had the most direct influence on church-state development in the United States, we will focus our historical survey on the Reformation development of church-state theory. Nevertheless, it is important to recognize the fact that the dual jurisdiction doctrine received its early affirmation and development in the Roman Catholic tradition. And since the Reformation, the official position of the Catholic Church has returned to a more Gelasian theory of church and state, one that recognizes the separate jurisdictions of church and state.[67]

ENGLISH LAW AND THE CHURCH

Before moving on to the Reformation, we must pause to consider important developments in England. Well before the Reformation, and indeed before the papal claims to supremacy were strongly embedded, Englishmen took firm hold of the dual jurisdictions doctrine. It eventually became embodied in practice in the common law.[68] In England, the emphasis was on the freedom of the church, rather than directly on the competing claims of papal versus royal supremacy. The principle was that the church should be free of the control of the state.

This principle was tested in a legendary showdown between King Henry II and Thomas Becket. Henry was a close friend of Becket, who was archdeacon of Canterbury. When the Archbishop of Canterbury died in 1162, Henry wanted Becket to take the position. Becket didn't want it. He warned Henry that if he got the position, he would have to be the advocate of the church even against Henry. Henry ignored the warning; Becket became archbishop, and kept his word. He resisted every attempt by Henry to infringe on the church's claimed jurisdiction.

Henry convened a council at Clarendon to settle the matter. The documents that came out of this council, the Constitutions of Clarendon, attempted to cut back legal privileges of the clergy. Thomas Becket relentlessly attacked them as an infringement on the church's rights. Henry was enraged by Becket's insolence, and it is reported that on one fateful night he angrily said, "Will no one rid me of this turbulent priest?"[69] Four of Henry's knights took him literally. They secretly traveled to Canterbury and killed Becket in the cathedral. While this appeared to be the ultimate breakdown of the independence of the church, the church won in the end. King Henry ultimately had to bear the responsibility, do penance, and renounce the offending portions of the Clarendon Constitutions.[70]

The importance of the dual jurisdictions view, and the extent to which it became embedded in the common law, can be seen in one of the most revered of common law documents, the Magna Charta (also spelled "Carta") of 1215.

King Richard the Lionheart had died, and his brother, John Lackland, was acting as king. As king, John outraged the nobility with his heavy-handed and capricious rule. Gathering an army of their retainers, the barons confronted King John at the meadow Runnymede with the demand that the king acknowledge the liberties and rights of Englishmen. John had no choice, and the document signed that day went down in history as the "Great Charter," or Magna Charta. For centuries after that, Magna Charta was viewed as a cornerstone of the English legal system. As the seventeenth century common law authority Sir Edward Coke put it, Magna Charta was "declaratory of the principall grounds of the fundamentall Laws of England."[71]

It is notable that the very first clause of this "Great Charter" proclaimed nothing less than the freedom and independence of the church:

> In the first place we have granted to God, and by this our present charter confirmed for us and our heirs forever, that the English church shall be free, and shall have its rights entire, and its liberties inviolate; and we will that it be thus observed . . . .

By the term "liberties," the document referred to the right of the English church to be governed ecclesiastically, without intervention from the civil rulers.[72]

Magna Charta thus began with the protection of the independence of the church from the state. Indeed, when the scholar Edward Coke attempted to distill the multifaceted document down to four basic purposes, the church figured prominently. The purposes of Magna Charta were, in Coke's words, "1. The honour of Almighty God, &c. 2. The safety of the Kings Soule; 3. The advancement of holy Church; and 4. The amendment of the Realme: foure most excellent ends . . . ."[73]

Magna Charta was of course not the only way that the common law acknowledged a distinction between the jurisdictions of church and state. Both in scholarly treatises and in the courts themselves, the jurisdictional distinctions were recognized.

Henry de Bratton, also known as Bracton, was a thirteenth century scholar and judge who systematized English law in the most influential legal treatise of its time.[74] Bracton recognized a distinction between the adjudication of "spiritual" and "temporal" matters and said that the common law courts were only competent to judge the latter.[75] "There is one jurisdiction . . . which pertains to the priesthood and the ecclesiastical forum . . . and another, ordinary or delegated, which pertains to the crown and dignity of the king and to the realm, in causes and pleas touching temporal things in the secular forum."[76]

As for the courts, according to legal scholar Herb Titus:

> For several centuries, English judges battled over
> whether cases involving marriage, tithes, inheritance
> of property, and the like were "temporal" or "spiritual."
> Whatever the merits of these claims and counterclaims,
> this principle was established: Some "wrongs" were not
> within the jurisdiction of the civil government courts
> that enforced the common law but were within the

jurisdiction of the ecclesiastical courts and vice versa; moreover, some wrongs were not within the jurisdiction of any human court.[77]

The English common law preserved the principle of dual jurisdictions at a time when the church leadership in Rome was abandoning that very principle. But there was still a need for a clear explanation of how the church and state should relate and interact, and what the authority structure precisely was. The Reformation would begin to answer these questions as it restored the theological perspective of church-state relations and articulated it with far greater precision than had been seen up to this point.

CHAPTER 2 IN A NUTSHELL...

- Augustine talks about two kingdoms, the "city of God" and the "city of man."
- Pope Gelasius talks about two jurisdictions, the church and the state.
- Medieval popes begin to place the church above the state.
- Meanwhile, English law comes to recognize two jurisdictions, church and state.

CHAPTER 3: THE REFORMATION OF CHURCH AND STATE

The Reformation shook Europe to the core. What began with an obscure theology professor in Germany challenging very specific abuses in the church soon expanded into a challenge of the authority of the Roman Church itself. This was a natural time to reconsider the authority of the church vis-à-vis the state, and indeed, the question of just what the relationship between the two should look like was soon being debated.

If we think of the church-state relationship as the proverbial pendulum, the challenge is to balance the pendulum in the middle, with co-equal authorities for church and state. The medieval Roman Catholic position had swung far toward the supremacy of the church over the state. The challenge of the Reformation was to bring the pendulum back to the middle. In doing so, there was a very real danger of overcompensating for the one extreme by taking the pendulum all the way to the other side, with the domination of the state over the church.[78]

ULRICH ZWINGLI

One of the first major reformers to reconsider church-state relations took such a "pendulum swing" position. Ulrich Zwingli became the first significant voice of the Reformation in Switzerland. A brilliant scholar of Scripture and a powerful communicator, Zwingli was also adept at networking with influential leaders who could advance the cause. This came to include the political leadership of the Swiss canton of Zurich, who became staunch supporters of the Reformed cause. Zwingli saw the Reformed magistrates as the proper counterweight to the Roman prelates. In doing so, he collapsed church and state into one nebulous Christian community: "When the gospel is preached and all, including the magistrate, heed it, the Christian man is nothing else than the faithful and good citizen; and the Christian city is nothing other than the Christian church."[79]

With this kind of thinking, it is not surprising that the magistrates in Zurich became involved in the process of church discipline itself. The churches could not excommunicate anyone without the permission of the town government. From Zwingli on, excommunication became one of the key indicators (though not the only indicator) of the status of a jurisdictional balance between church and state in the Reformation era. In general, if the church could exercise the ultimate ecclesiastical sanction—excommunication—on its own, the church was independent of the state. Church and state could each be "sovereign" within their respective "spheres." But if the state claimed the power to make the final decision on excommunication, the state was, in effect, claiming its sovereignty over the church itself.

Zwingli's views represented a pendulum swing away from church supremacy toward the direction of excessive state involvement. But other models of church and state were proposed by two of the leading Reformers, Martin Luther and John Calvin. They self-consciously attempted to balance the pendulum by recognizing real, distinct, and independent spheres of authority for church and state. Luther and Calvin set the tone for all that was to follow.

MARTIN LUTHER

Martin Luther was the obscure theology professor who posted a list of Latin theses on the door of All Saints' Church in Wittenburg in 1517 and initiated a theological revolution. In the series of controversies and confrontations that followed, Luther was forced to deal with issues that he could not have imagined facing when he originally nailed his Ninety-Five Theses to the church door.

Martin Luther's views of church and state were in many respects a return to the doctrines that Gelasius propounded some one thousand years earlier. Luther's influence on American law was not as direct Calvin's (who we shall consider shortly), but his contributions permeated the entire body of Reformation thought. A quick examination of Luther's positions will help us understand everything that followed.

First, Luther recognized the error of setting up a false dichotomy between the "sacred" and the "secular." He recognized two kingdoms, earth and heaven. But all people exist here on earth. The realm of heaven is God's. Thus, "there was no distinction between spiritual and temporal, sacred and secular work." [80] Luther came to recognize that all of life should be lived for the glory of God. [81] Rather than viewing society as some sort of spiritual hierarchy (a vertical perspective where the clergy are closer to God than the laity), Luther viewed society horizontally. In a "horizontal" society, there was "no person and no institution obstructed or mediated by any other in relationship to and accountability before God." [82]

From this recognition of society, institutions, and persons under God, Luther could see clearly that the church and the state were institutional equals. Here was another pair of two kingdoms, church and state. "For Luther, the relationship between the two kingdoms was parallel rather than hierarchical . . . . The Lutheran conception of the two kingdoms placed the temporal on roughly the same plane as the spiritual *vis-à-vis* the divine: the temporal was not subordinated to the spiritual." [83] As a result, God is over both church and state, even as church and state are distinct from each other. "In Lutheran theology, both the spiritual and the temporal kingdoms are God's; one is not 'more' the kingdom of God than the other, nor in this life is one assigned to rule over the other."[84] Both of the "two kingdoms" were ordained by God and under His authority. The church obviously was governed by "sola scriptura." In Lutheran thought, "The temporal realm remains God's creation and subject to God's law."[85]

In short, Luther recognized that two kingdoms existed here on earth. These two kingdoms, the state and the church, both have distinct jurisdictions. Neither could claim supremacy over the other, for both were equals before God.

Unfortunately, Luther did not fully flesh out this concept in practical terms.[86] He emphasized the distinction between the "church invisible" and the state but he did not devote much attention to the practical relationship between the local church (the "visible" church) and the state.[87] Luther's practical teachings emphasized the authority of the civil government more than the independence of the church.[88] In many Lutheran countries there ultimately came to be a very strong state influence on the practice of religion. Ironically, Luther's version of the "two kingdoms" eventually morphed into a new version of the very sacred-secular dichotomy that Luther himself wished to avoid. The kingdom of heaven became identified only with the spiritual, and the kingdom of earth identified only with the temporal.

Before going on, a comment on terminology is in order. The term "two kingdoms" is used by theologians and historians in two different ways. We can call it the "big tent" and the "little tent." In the big tent, it can refer to anyone who thinks about church and state in a jurisdictional way. Kuyper would be a believer in "two kingdoms" and so would Luther. Only someone like Zwingli, who would have let the church blur into the state and vice versa, would be excluded. But in the little tent, "two kingdoms theology" refers to a specific theological point. That point is that God's redemptive work is only going to occur through the church (and therefore efforts by Christians to redeem other institutions of culture are more or less misguided). Luther arguably had tendencies in this direction. Abraham Kuyper emphatically rejected it. (Kuyper insisted, "[T]here is not a square inch in the whole domain of our human existence over which Christ, who is Sovereign over *all*, does not cry: 'Mine!'"[89]) The debate over this kind of "two kingdoms" theology is really a debate over different kinds of Christian social engagement, not about church-state relations. In any case, it should be clear that we are focused primarily on the church-state relations. And when we encounter the term, "two kingdoms," in the future, we will attempt to make clear the sense in which the term is being used.

But meanwhile in Switzerland, another reformer was making the argument for distinct jurisdictions of church and state. He took parts of Luther's theology of church and state and ran with it in his own way.[90] This reformer made the arguments even more strongly and more systematically, and applied them in concrete terms to the visible institution of the local church.

JOHN CALVIN

Born in France in 1509, Calvin was a lad only eight years old when Luther wrote his 95 Theses. Calvin embraced the cause of Reformation as a young man, sometime in his early twenties. In 1535, at the young age of twenty-six, Calvin completed the first edition of his magnum opus, *The Institutes of the Christian Religion.* Even though he would continually revise this work throughout the rest of his life, its completion at such a young age is a remarkable achievement.[91] Calvin came to be most closely identified with Geneva, where he labored for the greater part of his life.

As far as influence on American law and philosophy goes, John

Calvin is arguably the most significant reformer.[92] The great church historian J.H. Merle d'Aubigné wrote that "Calvin was the founder of the greatest of republics. The Pilgrims who left their country in the reign of James I, and, landing on the barren shores of New England, founded populous and mighty colonies, are his sons; and that American nation which we have seen growing so rapidly boasts as its father the humble reformer."[93] The German historian Leopold von Ranke reportedly described Calvin as the virtual founder of America.[94] And the nineteenth century American historian George Bancroft wrote, "He that will not honor the memory, and respect the influence of Calvin, knows little of the origin of American liberty."[95] Some of these statements are overdramatic, but there certainly is truth in all of them.

Not all of the American founders were always conscious of the debt they owed Calvin, but at least some of them were. Specifically on the subject of church-state relations and religious freedom, John Adams wrote of the importance of Calvin's contributions, and it is worth quoting him at some length:

> After Martin Luther had introduced into Germany the liberty of thinking in matters of religion, and erected the standard of reformation, John Calvin, a native of Noyon, in Picardie, of a vast genius, singular eloquence, various erudition, and polished taste, embraced the cause of reformation. In the books which he published, and in the discourses which he held in the several cities of France, he proposed one hundred and twenty-eight articles in opposition to the creed of the Roman Catholic church. These opinions were soon embraced with ardor, and maintained with obstinacy, by a great number of persons of all conditions. The asylum and the centre of this new sect was Geneva, a city situated on the lake anciently called *Lemanus*, on the frontiers of Savoy, which had shaken off

the yoke of its bishop and the Duke of Savoy, and erected itself into a republic, under the title of a free city, for the sake of liberty of conscience. Let not Geneva be forgotten or despised. Religious liberty owes it much respect, Servetus notwithstanding. From this city proceeded printed books and men distinguished for their wit and eloquence, who spreading themselves in the neighboring provinces, there sowed in secret seeds of their doctrine. Almost all the cities and provinces of France began to be enlightened by it.[96]

Unfortunately, few people today are aware of the great contributions of Calvin. Those who are superficially acquainted with Calvin view him as the head of a theocracy in Geneva. It then comes as something of a shock to think of him as one of the key fathers of church-state separation. But his contributions were indeed great, and it is only to our loss if we fail to study the writings of this influential reformer. Calvin's time in Geneva is far more complex than the simplistic "theocracy" accusations commonly lodged against him.[97] We need to look past these caricatures so that we might more fully appreciate the theoretical contributions that Calvin made. Indeed, it could be said that one must understand John Calvin to understand the course of Western civilization; and if anything, this statement is even more applicable to the specific subject of church-state theory.

What makes Calvin doubly interesting for our purposes is that the practice of church discipline was closely tied to Calvin's thinking on church-state relations. A brief recounting of how this came to be will also help highlight how complicated Calvin's relationship with the city of Geneva really was.[98]

CHURCH DISCIPLINE AND THE GENEVAN CITY COUNCIL

When Calvin arrived in Geneva at the age of 27, he had no intention of remaining there for the rest of his life. But Farel, the leading Reformed minister in the city, convinced him that he was needed there, and the remarkably talented young Calvin quickly rose in popularity and prominence. He became the de facto spokesman for the reformed churches. But, rather like Luther, he was confrontational and was soon butting heads with the city council as he attempted to establish greater independence for the church.

Major controversy erupted over a number of proposals Calvin offered to the council on behalf of the Genevan ministers: implementing a regular schedule for administering communion, drafting a basic confession of faith, and giving the ministers the power to bar unrepentant sinners from receiving communion. The first proposal was worked out without too much trouble. The latter two caused considerable discord. The city council finally allowed the confession of faith but forbade the ministers from withholding communion from anyone. The council would not loosen its hold on the church's free exercise of discipline. Relations between the ministers and the council went downhill from there. New meddling by the council in church affairs led Calvin and other ministers to protest this violation of the independence of the church by refusing to celebrate communion on Easter 1538, and for this the city council banished the ministers. Calvin left Geneva for a pastorate in Strasburg.

In Calvin's absence, Geneva's churches were weak and the populace dissatisfied. The impotence of the remaining ministers was highlighted when the bishop Sadoleto appealed to the Genevans to return to the Roman church, for it was Calvin—still in exile—who wrote the defense of Protestantism on behalf of Geneva. When a more staunchly reformed contingent came to prominence on the city council, they began trying to persuade Calvin to return. It took a year before Calvin reluctantly gave in.

Calvin's first order of business upon returning to Geneva was to assert greater freedom for the church in a new set of ecclesiastical ordinances. Calvin viewed these ordinances as a step in the right direction, not the ideal. The ordinances allowed the city government more extensive power over the church than future Reformed churches would. For instance, the ministers finally had the power to nominate the men to be ordained as new ministers (which they had not had before), but the council still had the opportunity to review the decision. Calvin also avoided the issue of excommunication in the ordinances, apparently believing that the council was not yet ready to confront this issue head-on. Nonetheless, the ordinances accomplished their main objective: a new and vigorous church discipline began to be exercised without civil oversight. "For the body of the Church, to cohere well, must be bound together by discipline as with sinews," Calvin wrote.[99]

CALVIN, HERESY, AND THE STATE

What, then, of the old stereotype of the city rubber-stamping Calvin's decisions and persecuting heretics? Although Calvin viewed church and state as separate, it is true that he did believe that the two spheres should cooperate. In that capacity he had no qualms about reporting wrongdoing discovered by the church authorities to the civil authorities. And Calvin was very willing to use his personal influence in advising the council on any number of issues. But in fairness to Calvin, two considerations should be kept in sight. First, the degree of influence that Calvin possessed varied as his popularity and prestige went up and down. So Calvin never truly presided over a theocratic government.

Secondly, it should also be borne in mind that in the sixteenth century, heresy was universally viewed as an offense against the state, not just the church. So when the civil authorities punished heresy, it was not necessarily in violation of the principle of church-state separation, even though many today would think of these issues as church matters. To get a better perspective on this issue, imagine a chronic thief who is a church member. He could be subject to both church discipline and civil punishment, without violating the separation of church and state. The real issue with state heresy prosecutions was what crimes were within the domain of civil government, a distinct question from the basic principle of jurisdictional separation of church and state.

This does not mean that everything Calvin did was right or even consistent with his own stated views. But it does mean that we should not be too quick either to denounce him as a tyrant or discount him as a hypocrite.

CHURCH AND STATE IN CALVIN'S WRITINGS

With this background, we can now turn to Calvin's writings to learn what he had to say on the theology of church and state, which he addressed at considerable length.[100] He was concerned to avoid two extremes:

> [O]n the one hand, frantic and barbarous men are furiously endeavoring to overturn the order established by God [in the realm of civil government], and, on the other, the flatterers of princes, extolling their power without measure, hesitate not to oppose it to the government of God. Unless we meet both extremes, the purity of the faith will perish.[101]

In other words, Calvin believed that some Protestants were in danger of turning towards anarchy against civil government as they rejected the established order of things. This was a charge frequently leveled against the Reformed cause by Catholic polemicists, and Calvin was intent on refuting it. This was high on Calvin's list of priorities when he wrote the first edition of the *Institutes* as a young man. At the same time, Calvin was very concerned with the tendency of Zwingli's followers to elevate the civil government over the church. This naturally grew in importance to Calvin as he was forced to fight the Geneva city council for the independence of the church.

To those who did not believe in the need for church government, Calvin responded, "[T]he Church of God, as I have already taught, but am again obliged to repeat, needs a kind of spiritual government. This is altogether distinct from civil government ...."[102] To those who believed that new spiritual life eradicated the need for civil government, Calvin responded, "Christ's spiritual kingdom and the civil jurisdiction are things completely distinct."[103] In both cases, the jurisdictional separation of church and state was the basis of Calvin's response.

Calvin believed in a separation of the jurisdictions of church and state. In the words of one church historian, "[Calvin] made a clear distinction between church and state—institutionally, functionally and jurisdictionally—without separating Christianity from the state, which, equally with the church, is accountable to the triune God."[104]

In the *Institutes of the Christian Religion*, Calvin stated his belief that church discipline should "be altogether distinct from the power of the sword"[105]—that is, the power of civil government. He explained:

> Some ... are led astray, by not observing the distinc-
> tion and dissimilarity between ecclesiastical and civil
> power. For the Church has not the right of the sword
> to punish or restrain, has no power to coerce, no prison
> nor other punishments which the magistrate is wont to
> inflict. Then the object in view is not to punish the sinner
> against his will, but to obtain a profession of penitence
> by voluntary chastisement. The two things, therefore, are
> widely different, because neither does the Church assume
> anything to herself which is proper to the magistrate,
> nor is the magistrate competent to what is done by the
> Church.[106]

Calvin believed in an independent church supported and reinforced by a godly civil magistrate.[107] In this we see hints of a blending of roles, where church and state cooperate to maintain purity. This is what most observers think of first when they think of Calvin's contributions to church-state relations. But what is important is that even when Calvin speaks of the *cooperation* of church and state, he does not speak of the *subordination* of one to the other.

Calvin believed that the church and the state coexisted as two forms of government, separate and distinct from one another, but both under God and subject to His law and word. He explained, "As the magistrate ought by punishment and physical restraint to cleanse the church of offenses, so the minister of the Word should help the magistrate in order that fewer may sin. Their responsibilities should be so joined that each helps rather than impedes the other."[108] Calvin gave an example in the *Institutes* of what he meant by this:

> Does any one get intoxicated[?] In a well ordered city
> his punishment will be imprisonment. Has he commit-
> ted whoredom? The punishment will be . . . more severe.
> Thus satisfaction will be given to the [civil] laws, the mag-
> istrates, and the external tribunal. But the consequence
> will be, that the offender will give no signs of repentance,
> but will rather fret and murmur. Will the Church not
> here interfere?[109]

Thus, by the exercise of church discipline, the church assists the magistrate in his job of maintaining civil order. The church does not do this by some sort of joint church-state prosecution, however. Instead, it helps maintain order by bringing the offender to repentance in an *ecclesiastical* proceeding entirely separate from the civil proceeding.[110] This is not a merging of roles—the church does not commandeer the reigns of civil government, and the civil government does not dictate the exercise of church discipline. Thus, even in the sensitive issue of the church "aiding" the civil government, Calvin recognized a separation of jurisdictions.

CHURCH AND STATE ACROSS EUROPE

Calvin's influence was widespread in his own lifetime through his published writings and his extensive correspondences. Geneva became renowned as the model of a reformed city by many partisans of the Reformation across Europe. In the process, Calvin's ideas about the institutional separation of church and state were transmitted, studied, debated, and, in at least some cases, implemented by the Reformed churches across Europe.

MARTIN BUCER

In Calvin's own lifetime, some notable friends and colleagues echoed his perspectives on church discipline and jurisdictional roles of church and state. One such ally was Martin Bucer.

For many years, Bucer was a leader of the Protestant churches in Strasburg, with influence extending throughout Switzerland and Germany. His sphere of influence eventually came to encompass England as well, and he spent the final years of his life as a professor of theology at Cambridge. He became a good friend of John Calvin and maintained an active correspondence with the Genevan reformer. Bucer was actually the older of the two, and each influenced the other in their developing theologies.[111]

The recurring theme in Bucer's writings is the Lordship of Christ over every area of life.[112] He wrote that both the church and the state must equally submit themselves to the Lord. They then have distinct responsibilities here on earth. The magistrate has the responsibility to foster a well-ordered society under God, and the church has the more specific responsibility for administering the power of the "keys" (discipline and discipleship).[113] Bucer did not distinguish the roles as sharply as Calvin did,[114] but distinguish them he did. In his masterwork on church polity and discipline, he explained:

> [I]t is essential that over and above the general discipline
> of the civil authority, even if this is truly Christian and
> also diligent and zealous in applying punishment, the
> churches of Christ should have their own discipline and
> punishment: a discipline and punishment which are
> shown to be in the name, in the person, and on the behalf
> of Christ our Lord, with a clear and compelling reminder
> of God's severe judgment and the satisfaction of the
> Lord Jesus Christ for our sins: and also of the earnest and
> comforting command which he gave his church to bind
> and loose on earth, what was to be bound and loosed in
> heaven.[115]

PIERRE VIRET

On the issue of church-state separation, Calvin had an even more
important ally in Pierre Viret. Viret was one of the foremost preachers of
the Reformation and was also a prolific author of books on ethics, theology, and apologetics.[116] Viret preached all over Switzerland and spent time
ministering in Geneva, where he became one of Calvin's closest friends.[117]

Twenty-three years of Viret's ministry were spent in the Swiss canton
of Vaud, where he consistently struggled for the independence of the
church from the civil government authorities in Berne. The Reformation
had come to Berne after a public disputation convinced the magistrates
of the truth of the Reformed faith.[118] But this set the magistrates in the
dangerous position of dominance over church affairs.

Viret, for his part, "advocated a separation of church and state with
the church being responsible for its own government and discipline. This
tension over the delicate question of the relationship of ecclesiastical to

civil authority was the focal point around which each clash which Viret had with Berne was centered."[119]

Viret firmly believed in the independence of the church. Viret's biographers note that this was central to his work for many years. "Viret was often to declare that the Bernese Pope in short frock (the absolute State) was a far worse enemy for the faith than the old Pope of Rome in his long gown."[120] The question was "who really controlled the Reformed churches . . . , the secular government of Berne or the local ecclesiastical authorities?"[121] After more than two decades of controversy, the Bernese government finally banished Viret after he refused to submit church discipline to their authority.[122] For Viret, the proper jurisdictional control of the church, and specifically church discipline, was no mere side issue. He was willing to incur the wrath of the civil government to vindicate the principle of separate jurisdictions.

JURISDICTIONAL THINKING SPREADS

In France, the Huguenots came to support a jurisdictional separation of church and state. They even went so far as to prohibit magistrates from serving as elders in the churches, in order to avoid blurring the lines.[123]

In the Netherlands, the Synod of Dordrecht asserted the independence of the church, particularly in relation to church discipline.[124]

In the Palatinate of Germany, the issue was debated on and off throughout the 1560s and early 1570s. A church ordinance of 1564 instituted a system of magisterial oversight of church discipline (rather like that in Zwingli's Zurich) that troubled some of the pastors who agreed with Calvin that church discipline needed to be independent of the state. An English student at the great Reformed university at Heidelberg finally set off the large-scale debating by proposing as a thesis for debate that independent church discipline was a necessary mark of a true church. A professor of medicine named Thomas Erastus opposed independent discipline and instead advocated the subordination of the church to the state. The advocates of free and independent church discipline (known as the *Disziplinisten*) won out in 1571. But a manuscript Erastus wrote defending state control over the church would come back to fuel further controversy later in England, where once again the doctrine of separate jurisdictions confronted the idea of state control.

CHAPTER 3 IN A NUTSHELL...

- The Reformation leads to a reexamination of the relationship between church and state.
- Zwingli puts the state over the church.
- Luther and Calvin recognize church and state as equals.
- Calvin wants the church to have the ability to exercise church discipline, free from the control of the government.
- The understanding that church and state are distinct jurisdictions spreads in the areas influenced by Calvin's teaching.

CHAPTER 4: CHURCH AND STATE IN THE SCOTTISH AND ENGLISH REFORMATIONS

For purposes of understanding the American legal heritage on church-state relations, the experiences of the Scottish and English Reformation are all too often neglected. But as we turn to them now, we shall see that they provide a backdrop for the American constitutional experiment. The experiences and debates that occurred over the span of a century were woven together into a rich and diverse tapestry of perspectives on church-state relations. It could hardly be otherwise, given the fact that in England the reform of the church was directly connected with the whim of the king.

The Reformation in England got off to an inauspicious start under the brilliant but capricious King Henry VIII. In 1521, Henry wrote a treatise defending the seven sacraments of the Roman Catholic Church and attacking Martin Luther as a servant of Satan. No one at this point would have guessed that Henry would within a few years initiate England's official break with Rome. To the contrary, Pope Leo X was impressed with Henry's work in defense of Rome and gave him the title, "Defender of the Faith" (still retained by the English monarchy). Leo's successor, Pope Clement VII, was so enamored of the king's defense of Catholic doctrine that he promised an indulgence to all who read the book.[125]

But Henry soon had personal problems with the Roman Church. He wanted a son as an heir and he wanted Anne Boleyn as his wife. Queen Catherine was in the way on both counts. To divorce Catherine, Henry needed approval from the pope, but he couldn't get it.

After four years of political and ecclesiastical maneuvering, Henry was infuriated with the pope's recalcitrance. "What!," he wrote, "must a prince submit to the arrogance of a human being whom God has put under him? Must a king humble himself before that man above whom he stands by the will of God? No! that would be a perversion of the order God has established."[126] No separate spheres existed in Henry's mind. Either the church was above the king, or the king was over the church. Not surprisingly, when Henry made the fateful decision to break with Rome, he declared himself to be head of the church.

The switch from the supremacy of church over state to the supremacy of state over church concerned many of the Reformed leaders. But so did much else in the Church of England (most especially the ceremonies and hierarchy that the Church of England retained from its Roman predecessor). The most serious and lengthy discussion over the church-state issue in England would not come until decades later, during the tumultuous Civil War era. In the interim, though, we need to turn our attention northward, for important events were happening in Scotland on the church-state issue. Once again, church discipline issues played into the controversy.

JOHN KNOX

The Scottish Reformation's leading figure, the remarkable John Knox, spent several formative years in Calvin's Geneva and was familiar with Calvin's positions. But no mere clone, Knox and, even more importantly, his successors in the leadership of the reformed church in Scotland made important and unique contributions to our heritage on church-state relations. The eminent nineteenth century Scottish author Thomas Carlyle remarked that John Knox is "the one Scotchman to whom, of all others, his country and the world owe a debt."[127] We will spend some time on Knox, giving a quick overview of his tumultuous life, before we return to his contributions to church discipline and, ultimately, church-state relations.

Today, unfortunately, Knox is largely known not for his work on behalf of the church, but as a caricatured fire-breathing prophet figure who wanted to persecute anyone who would not agree with him. But prophets are often misunderstood, maligned, or marginalized by those who are opposed to their work, and such is the case with Knox. The writer Thomas Carlyle memorably captured the human side of Knox:

> They go far wrong who think this Knox was a gloomy, spasmodic, shrieking fanatic. Not at all; he is one of the solidest men; a most shrewd, observing, quietly discerning man; an honest-hearted, brotherly man—brother to the high, brother also to the low: sincere in his sympathy with both; a cheery, social man with faces that loved him. An ill nature he decidedly had not. Kind, honest, affections dwelt in the much-enduring, hard-worn, ever-battling man. Close at hand, he was found to be no mean, acrid man, but at heart a healthful, strong sagacious man.[128]

John Knox was born in either 1514 or 1515 near the village of Haddington, Scotland.[129] In 1536, after studying at the University of St. Andrews, he was ordained a Roman Catholic priest. He was unable to make a living because of the large number of priests in Scotland at the time, and so he tried his hand at practicing law in 1540. His work as a lawyer did not last long and he changed course in 1543 when he accepted a position as a tutor for children in two homes. Both of these families were active in the fledgling Reformation movement in Scotland. It was at this time in his life, exposed to the doctrines of the Reformation, that Knox was converted. History has not preserved the details of this important event, other than Knox's recollection that it came about through his study of John 17.[130]

After his conversion, John Knox met the Reformed preacher George Wishart when he came through Edinburgh in 1544, preaching justification by faith. Wishart was a wanted man—Cardinal Beaton put a price on Wishart's head and tried several times to have him assassinated.[131] But Knox developed a close friendship with Wishart, voluntarily putting himself into harm's way by becoming Wishart's bodyguard. Knox would carry a broad sword in order to protect Wishart as he preached the gospel.[132] Wishart, knowing that his martyrdom was near, asked Knox to leave him, assuring Knox that one sacrifice would be quite sufficient.[133]

Reluctantly, Knox parted ways with Wishart, and his mentor was captured and burned at the stake outside the Castle of St. Andrews. In retaliation for Wishart's death, a band of Protestant belligerents stormed Cardinal Beaton's chambers and assassinated him.[134] Though Knox did not condone the act, he was glad for Beaton's death,[135] and thereafter joined other Protestants in the Castle (now a Protestant stronghold), bringing with him three Reformed students he was tutoring.[136]

While at St. Andrews, Knox answered the call to preach and thundered for the purity of the Gospel with marked zeal. Contemporaries who knew both Wishart and Knox characterized the younger reformer as more outspoken than his bold elder. One contemporary commented, "Others lop off the branches of Papistry, but [Knox] striketh at the root also, to destroy the whole." Another warned, "Master George [Wishart] spake never so plainly; and yet he was burnt. Even so will John Knox be."[137]

In August of 1547, the Castle of St. Andrews fell to a force of eighteen French galleons who attacked the fortress from the sea. Knox and his comrades were taken as prisoners, and Knox spent the next nineteen months as a galley slave, chained to the oars of a French ship. He was mercifully released—alive—in February of 1549.[138]

By this time, Henry VIII was dead, and a committed Protestant, the young Edward VI, was on the throne of England. Knox saw England, the southern rival to his native land, as offering a better prospect for reform,[139] so he headed to England. He took up a pastorate in Berwick for two years before assuming the same role in Newcastle. Next, he was appointed an official chaplain to Edward VI in London.[140] While in England, Knox helped revise the Book of Common Prayer and the Church of England's Articles of Religion (later known as the 39 Articles).[141]

In the summer of 1553, King Edward VI died and an ardent Roman Catholic, Mary Tudor, ascended to the throne. The new queen, later to be known as "Bloody Mary," quickly began her reign of terror against the Puritans. Many were martyred, including Thomas Cranmer, the Archbishop of Canterbury. Knox managed to evade the government agents searching for him and fled to Geneva in January 1554. The city was a bastion of Reformed thought and Knox took advantage of the op- portunity to work with and learn from like-minded theologians, includ- ing John Calvin.

On his return to Scotland and during the tumultuous time surround- ing the Queen Regent's death in 1560, Knox made his most significant contributions to church-state ideas. Drawing on Calvin's *Ordinances* from his church in Geneva, Knox was the primary drafter of two signifi- cant documents, a *Confession of Faith* and a *Book of Discipline*. The *Book of Discipline* was a plan for church organization and government.[142]

KNOX ON CHURCH DISCIPLINE AND JURISDICTIONS

Although the *Book of Discipline* was not officially adopted for the Scottish church, many of the Scottish Reformed congregations began to use it. Knox, for his part, continued to preach "that we should constantly proceed to reform all abuses, and to plant the ministry of the church, as by God's Word we might justify it, and then commit the success of all to our God in whose power the disposition of the true kingdom stands."[143] Knox's passion was to promote a biblical, well-ordered church.

John Calvin, Knox's friend and mentor, said, "Wherever we see the Word of God purely preached and heard, and the sacraments administered according to Christ's institution, there, it is not to be doubted, a church of God exists." Knox would agree and then add a third mark to the definition of a biblical church: "ecclesiastical discipline uprightly ministered, as God's Word prescribes, whereby vice is repressed and virtue nourished."[144] In other words, church discipline was an essential mark of a biblical Reformed church, in Knox's view. But he also urged the church to use discipline to restore the sinner, not to punish him. He recognized that the true purpose of church discipline was repentance and restoration of the sinner to Christ and His church. (This should challenge our contemporary notions that Knox or any of the Reformed leaders in Scotland wanted to cut off all who disagreed with them.)

How, then, did this relate to church-state issues? Does the church operate above the state, as the Roman Catholic Church taught? Does the state operate above the church, as Henry VIII would have it? Or are both coequal under God, with distinct jurisdictions? Knox joined Calvin in holding that the two are distinct, with different areas of competence. In the *Book of Discipline*, Knox explained why there was a necessity for church discipline:

> As no commonwealth can flourish or long endure without good laws, and sharp execution of the same, so neither can the Kirk [church] of God be brought to purity, neither yet be retained in the same, without the order of ecclesiastical discipline, which stands in reproving and correcting of those faults which the civil sword either doth neglect or may not punish.[145]

In other words, Knox and the Scottish reformers believed that there were certain wrongs or "faults" that the civil jurisdiction may not punish precisely because those wrongs were outside the civil sphere of authority. Church and state both have legitimate authority, but directed to different spheres.

ANDREW MELVILLE AND THE SECOND BOOK OF DISCIPLINE

During John Knox's lifetime, the Reformation in Scotland was the scene of constant church-state conflicts. The civil government itself was divided over the Reformation. Catholic Queen Mary Stuart vigorously opposed the Reformation (and was famously rebuked by Knox). The Scottish Parliament supported the Reformation in varying degrees.[146] But even after Mary's forced abdication in 1567, conflicts continued as the church's General Assembly struggled with Parliament over the control of church property.[147]

Into this chaos stepped Andrew Melville, Knox's most important successor in leading the Scottish reformed church. Perhaps more than any other, Melville was responsible for Scotland's general adoption of Presbyterian rather than Episcopal church government.[148] Melville authored the *Second Book of Discipline*, adopted by the General Assembly in 1578, specifically to deal with the problem of church-state relations. The document begins, explains Scottish historian Thomas McCrie,

> by laying down the essential line of distinction between civil and ecclesiastical power. Jesus Christ, it declares, has appointed a government in his church, distinct from civil government . . . . Civil authority has for its . . . object the promoting of external peace and quietness among the subjects, ecclesiastical authority, the directing of men in matters of religion and which pertain to conscience; the former enforces obedience by external means, the latter by spiritual means; yet . . . they "both be of God . . . ."[149]

As another historian put it: "*The [Second] Book* postulated the existence of two parallel, divinely ordained jurisdictions, separate and distinct, yet co-ordinate. The phraseology of the 'two kingdoms' was not employed to describe the relationship, but the implication was there."[150]

MELVILLE VERSUS THE KING

The doctrine of two kingdoms was anathema to the young King James VI of Scotland. James had been raised by Presbyterian tutors, but preferred a more hierarchical system of church government. It fit better with his philosophy of the divine right of kings.

Not surprisingly, King James, with his expansive ideas of royal power, also favored the supremacy of the king over the church. This doctrine became known as Erastianism, after Thomas Erastus, the Swiss academic who argued for state supremacy during the debates in the Palatinate.[151] "[The] 'Erastian' view . . . taught that, in a Christian state, the chief magistrate ought to be the head of the church as well as of the state and that, consequently, there should be no independent ecclesiastical government or discipline. The government of the church should be co-terminus with and subsumed under that of the state."[152] Henry VIII of England had already asserted a similar view when he declared himself the head of the Church of England, and so it was not surprising that James, a brilliant but egotistical monarch, would latch onto the Erastian position.

Melville confronted this issue directly in a 1596 meeting with the young King James. An early biographer of Melville records that Melville tactlessly caught the king by the sleeve, addressed him as "God's sillie vassal,"[153] and continued:

> Therefore, sir, as divers times before I have told you, so now again I must tell you, there are two kings and two kingdoms in Scotland: there is King James, the head of this commonwealth, and there is Christ Jesus, the King

of the Church, whose subject James the Sixth is, and of whose kingdom he is not a king, nor a lord, nor a head, but a member. We will yield to you your place, and give you all due obedience; but again I say, you are not the head of the Church . . . .[154]

THE *PROTESTATION*

The Church of Scotland continued to draw sharp lines between the king's authority and the church's authority in its contest against King James' son, Charles I. As one historian put it, James was enough of a statesman to avoid disaster; Charles was not.[155] As the situation in England spiraled out of control and toward civil war, Charles persisted in attempting to impose Anglican modes of worship on unwilling Scots, with disastrous consequences.

In November of 1638, the General Assembly of the Church of Scotland met with 150 ministers and 98 elders who were determined to resist Charles I's attempts to impose the Anglican establishment upon them. They defied instructions from the King's High Commissioner, the Marquis of Hamilton, to dissolve their Assembly. It was Hamilton who presented the Assembly with a new "covenant" drafted by the king. The Assembly, which was made up of such notable men as Alexander Henderson, George Gillespie, and Samuel Rutherford,[156] rejected the king's edict. The Assembly published a document titled, *The Protestation of the Generall Assemblie of the Church of Scotland*. The *Protestation* declared its sole dependence upon Christ's crown and announced its independence from the crown of the English king. The *Protestation*, drafted by Alexander Henderson, boldly stated:

It was most unnatural in itself and prejudicial to the privileges which Christ in His word, has left to His church to dissolve or break up the assembly of this church, or

to stop and stay their proceedings in constitution of acts
for the welfare of the church or execution of discipline
of offenders and so to make it appear that religion and
church government should depend upon the pleasure of
the prince.[157]

This important document, written at a pivotal time in English and
Scottish history, clearly was based on an institutional and jurisdictional
separation of the church from the state.

One of the other authors of the *Protestation* would go on to become one of the greatest advocates for a jurisdictional understanding
of church and state in England itself. This was George Gillespie, who
went to England as one of Scotland's commissioners to the Westminster
Assembly. Gillespie died in 1648 at the young age of 35, but in his short
life, he became renowned for his scholarship and learning.[158] His major
work was called *Aaron's Rod Blossoming*, a treatise that is one of the defini-
tive works on the biblical doctrine of the separation of church and state.
Gillespie wrote this work to confront the English (Erastian) view that a
Christian civil magistrate should be the head of the church.[159]

In denying this view, Gillespie argued, "The controversy is not about
taking from the magistrate what is his, but about giving to Christ that
which is his. We hold a reciprocal subordination of persons, but a co-
ordination of powers."[160] Gillespie rooted his argument for church and
state as separate jurisdictions in the Old Testament's division of power
between civil and ecclesiastical realms:

The Jewish church was formally distinct from the Jewish
state. I say formally, because ordinarily they were not distinct materially, the same persons being members of both;
but formally they were distinct, as now the church and the
state are among us Christians.[161]

SCOTLAND AND ENGLAND MEET

While theologians like Gillespie worked to articulate a biblical approach to church-state relations, political events in England were spiraling out of control. The English Parliament was fed up with the authoritarian rule of King Charles (who, like his father, believed in "divine right" kingship). The dispute between king and Parliament degenerated into civil war. Although there were many reasons for the war, the dispute between the king and the Puritans was certainly a potent part of the mix. And the theological issues came to play an important role when the English Parliament sought to make an alliance with Scotland.

This alliance was in part a theological alliance. In 1643, Parliament asked for a meeting of church leaders to work on a confession of faith. This meeting brought together Scottish and English divines for what came to be known as the Westminster Assembly. Part of the objective was to lay out an improved plan for "discipline and government in the church."[162]

There was heated controversy over the exact form of church government and its relationship to civil government. While the Scots in the Assembly (including Gillespie himself) championed independence for the church, not all of the English delegates were ready for such a radical move. There was a small but vocal Erastian group in the English delegation that wanted church discipline to be entirely subject to the civil government (effectively taking church discipline away from the church).[163] Parliament also had to have its say. The Scots ended up disappointed that the church's authority to exercise church discipline, among other things, was not severed from the civil sphere. The Scots viewed this as a compromise with Erastianism.[164]

Still, in the Westminster Confession itself, the advocates of jurisdictional separation won an important victory. Chapter XXIII of the Confession discusses the civil magistrate, and it does so in a way that acknowledges the separation of jurisdictions between church and state:

God, the Supreme Lord and King of all the world, hath
ordained civil magistrates to be under him over the
people, for his own glory and the public good; and to this
end, hath armed them with the power of the sword, for
the defense and encouragement of them that are good,
and for the punishment of evil-doers. . . . The civil magistrate may not assume to himself the administration of
the Word and sacraments, or the power of the keys of the
kingdom of heaven . . . .[165]

THE ENGLISH PURITANS ON CHURCH AND STATE

While Scotland seemed to provide much of the leadership for
advancing a "two kingdoms" view of church and state, there were
Englishmen who caught the vision. The Puritan movement was the
vehicle in England that had confronted first King James and then King
Charles with their concerns for the purity and continued reformation of
the English church. The headship of the king over the church came to
be one of the great concerns of many Puritans. A Puritan, according to
historian Iain Murray, was "a man ready to suffer not only for the gospel
but for Christ's right to rule the church by his own authority."[166]

A desire for biblical church discipline free of state control was one
of the major motivations for the Puritans. As early as 1572, the nascent
Puritan movement raised this issue in an "Admonition to the Parliament,"
where they complained that it was inappropriate to have "civill offices,
joyned to the Ecclesiasticall, it is againste the worde of God."[167]

The very first confrontation between the Puritans and King James
involved this issue. James was on his way from Scotland to London after
his accession to the English throne in the spring of 1603. A group of divines presented him with a petition signed by almost a thousand pastors,
a document which came to be known as the "Millenary Petition." The

petition listed a number of the grievances that the Puritans had against the Church of England.[168] Among them was a request "For Church discipline: that the discipline and excommunication may be administered according to Christ's own institution . . . ." The document specifically objected to state control of church discipline, requesting that "excommunication come not forth under the name of lay persons, chancellors, officials, &c . . . ."[169] James rejected the demands of the Puritans in the Hampton Court Conference in January 1604. After hearing the disputes between the bishops and the Puritan pastors, James said of the Puritans, "If this be all they have to say, I will make them conform themselves, or harry them out of the land."[170]

The church discipline and church-state relations that were at issue in the very first confrontation with James as king of England never disappeared throughout the years following, as the struggle between the Puritans and the monarchy continued.[171] As the English Puritans joined forces with their Scottish Presbyterian allies, they continued to articulate the principles of church discipline and separate jurisdictions for church and state (notably in the Westminster Confession, as we have seen).

The brilliant polymath theologian Richard Baxter was considered one of the leading Puritan theologians of his time, and he articulately explained the separate jurisdictions for church and state. Born in England on November 12, 1615, Baxter was ordained in the Church of England. But "Baxter held that the episcopacy as it had been practiced in the Church of England, with autocratic prelates lording it over unduly large dioceses, badly needed reform."[172] In 1659, Baxter published his most famous and controversial book, *A Holy Commonwealth*. Baxter wrote, "God doth not communicate all that Power in kind which is Eminently and Transcendently in himself to any one man, or sort of Officers; but distributeth to each their part; Civil Power to Civil Rulers, and Ecclesiastical to Church-Rulers."[173] This was, of course, a succinct and direct statement of the jurisdictional view of church and state.

CHAPTER 4 IN A NUTSHELL...

- John Knox leads the Reformation in Scotland.
- Knox teaches that the church needs authority to practice church discipline without state interference.
- The English Puritans agree with Knox.
- King James and King Charles believe that the state is above the church.
- The Puritan struggle with James and Charles leads to the English Civil War.

CHAPTER 5: CHURCH AND STATE IN AMERICA: THE REFORMATION HERITAGE

The first English settlements were planted in America shortly after James I ascended the English throne. The English settlers brought with them a strong Protestant heritage, including the Reformed understanding of church and state.

Most people today are surprised to hear that there was any degree of separation between church and state in colonial America. Too often, we in modern America have viewed the early settlement era solely as one of established churches and the suppression of dissent. Then Thomas Jefferson and James Madison seem to walk onto the stage of history out of nowhere, with new and novel ideas about the state being separate from the church. But whenever ideas seem to arrive out of thin air, there is reason to be suspicious. This picture is not fair to those who came before, including the (much-maligned) Puritans. The Puritans laid many important foundations that bore fruit in the new nation after independence,[174] so much so that Alexis de Tocqueville, the great observer of early America, called the Puritans the true founders of America.[175]

This is not to say that the early colonial era was without problems. It is important to emphasize that none of the preservers of "two kingdoms" theory were perfect, and for many of them, serious inconsistencies existed between their theory and practice. These are often glaringly obvious to modern historians with the benefit of hindsight. The problem is that in pointing out inconsistencies and errors in the past, we miss the nuggets of gold that they have to give us—insight into issues that they understood much better than we have. Although state churches were established in many of the colonies, the seeds of the two-jurisdictions doctrine were far from dead in colonial America.

THE PILGRIMS AND PURITANS

The "Pilgrims" who founded the Plymouth colony had a particularly personal (negative) experience with state intervention in the church, and their settlement helped to lay the foundations for jurisdictional thinking about church and state. The Pilgrims were better known in their own time as "Separatists," a radical subgroup of Puritans who wanted to separate completely from what they saw as the unbiblical practices of the established Church of England. Several of their congregations left England for Holland because of the intrusion of the state into their local assembly in the form of arrests and imprisonment of church leaders. One of their leaders, William Bradford, recorded their plight:

> Yet seeing themselves thus molested, and that there was no hope of their continuance there, by a joint consent resolved to go into the Low Countries, where they heard was freedom of religion for all men; as also how sundry from London and other parts of the land. So after they had continued together about a year, and kept their meetings every Sabbath in one place or other, exercising the worship of God amongst themselves, notwithstanding all the diligence and malice of their adversaries, they seeing they could no longer continue in that condition, they

resolved to get over into Holland as they could. Which
was in the year 1607 and 1608 . . . .[176]

When these Separatists made a petition to King James in 1609, it
was rich in the terminology of jurisdictional thinking about church and
state.[177] It was this group of Separatists, concerned about keeping the
state from controlling the church, who set sail for America a decade later
(for which they became known as "Pilgrims").

The Pilgrims were the first of what turned out to be a growing migra-
tion of Puritans to the Massachusetts Bay area over the next twenty years.
Later in the 1620s, the Massachusetts Bay Colony was established by
more mainstream (non-separatist) Puritans. There was a massive influx
of Puritans throughout the next decade, and probably 20,000 immigrated
by 1642.[178]

The Massachusetts colony may not have always fulfilled the two-
jurisdictions ideal, but it was still frequently articulated there. The
Massachusetts Body of Liberties (1641) established limits on the authority of the civil authorities to be involved in church government. It
provided that the magistrates could protect the peace and order of the
churches so long as "it be done in a Civill and not in an Ecclesiastical
way."[179] No less notable a New England minister than John Cotton wrote
in 1645 of the difference between the powers of the church in exercising
discipline (the "power of the keys"), and the powers of the state in administering justice (the "power of the sword"): "The power of the keys is far
distant from the power of the sword, and though one of them may need
the helpe of the other, when they goe astray, yet when they are rightly ordered, and administered, the one of them doth not intercept, but establish
the execution of the other."[180]

When we think of church discipline among the Massachusetts Bay
Puritans, we often think of legalistic churches banishing their enemies
from the colony. While there were situations where this happened, it was
the exception rather than the rule. Usually discipline was done for the

biblical purpose of restoration, not for punishment. A leading historian of the Puritans recently wrote, "In most of the recorded cases excommunication had the desired result; the sinner did repent and was readmitted into the church."[181]

During the years of 1646 and 1648 representatives of the Congregational churches of Massachusetts met in Cambridge to draw up a book of church order. The Congregational churches did not subscribe to the Presbyterian polity of the newly drafted Westminster Confession, and they wanted to draft a specifically Congregational document that would prescribe how the churches should relate to one another. Out of this synod of churches came The Cambridge Platform[182] of 1649, largely the work of John Cotton, Richard Mather, and Ralph Partridge. The Cambridge Platform outlined various aspects of the government, order, and discipline of the church. According to historians Daniel Dreisbach and Mark Hall, the Platform "illustrates the Congregationalists' view of the proper relationship between individuals and churches, churches and churches, and church and state."[183]

The Platform may have differed from the Westminster Confession on issues of church order, but it was in entire agreement on the jurisdictional separation of church and state. It explicitly stated that church discipline was an entirely "ecclesiastical" punishment. It cannot deprive anyone of his "civil rights": "Excommunication being a spiritual punishment, it doth not prejudice the excommunicate in, nor deprive him of his civil rights, and therefore touches not princes or magistrates in respect of their civil dignity or authority."[184] In the discussion "Of the Civil Magistrate's Power in Matters Ecclesiastical" the authors made it very clear that it was "not in the power of magistrates to compel their subjects to become church members, and to partake of the Lord's Table."[185]

Thus, the New England Puritans repeatedly stated their belief in an institutional separation of church and state.[186] The civil sphere must remain in its properly delineated role and the ecclesiastical sphere must keep to things spiritual and not "civil." The New England ideal remained independent, covenanted congregations, with "the keys of heaven . . . administered by the local congregation and the civil sword . . . administered by the colonial Governor and the magistrates."[187]

While the colonies became increasingly diverse over the next century, the majority of the colonists were of the Reformed stripe, familiar with the "two kingdoms" perspective.[188] In practice, the jurisdictional perspective was seriously diluted by the formal legal establishment of particular denominations in many colonies.[189] But the practical implications of the jurisdictional perspective would be revived and reinvigorated in the new nation after the Revolution.

THE SCOTTISH MIGRATIONS

The New England Calvinists brought the basic principles of two kingdoms with them in their theology, but an equally important (perhaps an even more important) influence came from another group that immigrated in even larger numbers. These were Scots and the so-called "Scotch Irish," Scottish Presbyterians who had relocated to Ulster in the early 1600s.[190] Their immigration to the American colonies takes us from the seventeenth century all the way up to the beginnings of the War for Independence.

Beginning in the 1680s, Scottish Covenanters began immigrating to America to escape a new wave of persecution under James II.[191] This first group was followed by a wave of Scotch-Irish immigrants in 1717, then four more waves of immigration, the last occurring from 1771 to 1775.[192] On the eve of the War for Independence, there was a mass influx. Between 1760 and 1775, approximately 40,000 Scots and 55,000 Protestant Irish immigrated.[193] These numbers by themselves amounted to an amazing 3% of the entire population of Scotland in 1760, and 2.3% of the Irish population.[194] By 1775, it is estimated that there were about

900,000 Scotch-Irish in America, out of a total population of roughly three million.[195] These immigrants created a strong citizen base saturated in the Scottish Presbyterian version of "two kingdoms" theology. By the time of the American War for Independence, approximately two-thirds of the American population was comprised of non-Anglican (dissenting) groups,[196] the majority of which had a Calvinist theological orientation.[197] It is not surprising then that the Reformation heritage of "two kingdoms" had an influence on the legal questions of church-state relations immediately following the War for Independence.

JOHN WITHERSPOON AND THE AMERICAN PRESBYTERIANS

Included in the number of Scottish Presbyterians immigrating to America was John Witherspoon, a pastor who arrived in 1768. John Witherspoon was born into a family with a long history of clergymen (reportedly descended from John Knox himself).[198] He was a brilliant student, taught first by his mother, then at a local grammar school. He went off to the university in Edinburgh at the ripe old age of 13. He graduated with his doctorate at age 20 and entered into the ministry. As a pastor, theologian, and writer, his fame spread far and wide—including to the American colonies, where the College of New Jersey (now Princeton University) was searching for a new president. Two eminent Princeton men (both future signers of the Declaration of Independence) convinced Witherspoon—and just as importantly, his wife Elizabeth—that his place was at the College of New Jersey.[199]

In the position of college president, Witherspoon became a well-known advocate of independence, was elected to Congress, and signed the Declaration of Independence.[200] Perhaps most importantly, Witherspoon personally taught many of the leading statesmen of his time then they were young men studying under him at Princeton. These students included 3 Supreme Court justices, 20 senators, 33 U.S. representatives, 10 cabinet members, 12 governors, and 114 ministers. James

Madison, architect of the Constitution and future president, also came to Princeton and personally studied under Witherspoon.[201]

What did Witherspoon believe about church and state? Did he really import a Scottish Presbyterian theology of church and state? There is evidence he did.

At the same time as the U.S. Constitution was being discussed and ratified in the colonies (1787–89), the Presbyterian Church in America set about to unify its confession of faith. The Presbyterian convention, under the leadership of John Witherspoon, made several modifications to their creed, the Westminster Confession of 1647.[202] Of special significance was the change made to the section on the civil magistrate.

The original wording of the confession acknowledged the jurisdictional distinctions between church and state when it stipulated that "[t]he civil magistrate may not assume to himself the administration of the Word and sacraments, or the power of the keys of the kingdom of heaven."[203] Yet it still recognized authority in the civil magistrate to define doctrine, suppress all "blasphemies and heresies," and ensure that "the ordinances of God" be "duly . . . administered."[204] The magistrate was also granted the power "to call synods, to be present at them, and to provide, that whatsoever is transacted in them be according to the mind of God."[205]

The American Presbyterians retained the opening clause prohibiting the civil magistrate from assuming the administration of the "keys of the kingdom." But they dramatically reworded the rest of the section. The language granting the civil magistrate power to punish heresies was removed. The new emphasis was placed on the magistrate protecting the church while prohibiting the state from interfering with matters of the church.

> [A]s nursing fathers,[[206]] it is the duty of civil magistrates
> to protect the Church of our common Lord, without

giving the preference to any denomination of Christians above the rest, in such a manner that all ecclesiastical persons whatever shall enjoy the full, free, and unquestioned liberty of discharging every part of their sacred functions, without violence or danger. And, as Jesus Christ hath appointed a regular government and discipline in his Church, no law of any commonwealth should interfere with, let, or hinder, the due exercise thereof, among the voluntary members of any denomination of Christians, according to their own profession and belief.[207]

If there was any doubt remaining as to the intent of the American Presbyterians, Witherspoon dispelled it by authoring the Introduction to the 1789 edition of the Westminster Confession of Faith.[208] In this introduction, he drove home the separation of the two distinct spheres, civil and religious:

That "God alone is Lord of the conscience, and hath left it free from the doctrines and commandments of men; which are in anything contrary to his word, or beside it in matters of faith or worship." Therefore, the synod reassert [*sic*] the rights of private judgment in matters of religion, repudiate all ties to the civil government, and call for full freedom of religion for all.[209]

These changes brought the creed into greater conformity with the Scottish—and now, American—understanding of the role of the civil magistrate as it relates to ecclesiastical matters. It was a broader conception of church autonomy than before, but it was not revolutionary; it was a natural progression in theological history. It was simply further refining the theology of jurisdictions of church and state.

JAMES MADISON AND THE *MEMORIAL AND REMONSTRANCE*

After the American Revolution, the relationship between church and state became an issue in many states. The Anglican Church lost its position as the legally-favored (or "established") church in more and more states.[210] The most famous debate about church and state from this era comes from Virginia, the largest state of the new nation. A bill "Establishing a Provision for Teachers of the Christian Religion" was introduced in the Virginia House of Delegates in 1784.[211] The non-Anglican dissenters—particularly the Baptists[212]—saw this as a threat to their freedom, since the Anglican church would be the default recipient of benefits from the bill.[213] Through alliances with powerful figures like James Madison, the Baptists and other dissenters successfully defeated the bill.[214] In the process, the debate over this bill resulted in what is arguably the most significant, and certainly the most famous, statement of church-state relations in the early republic, Madison's *Memorial and Remonstrance*.

Although James Madison made his arguments in *Memorial and Remonstrance* in terms of individual liberties (religious freedom) rather than institutional jurisdictions (ecclesiastical autonomy), he employed a rationale similar to that used to defend the independence of the church. First, Madison explained, it needs to be recognized that civil society is under God: "[E]very man who becomes a member of any particular Civil Society . . . [does it yet reserving] his allegiance to the Universal Sovereign."[215] Because of this, "We maintain . . . that in matters of religion no man's right is abridged by the institution of Civil Society, and that religion is wholly exempt from its cognizance."[216]

Madison continued, reasoning that "if religion be exempt from the authority of the society at large, still less can it be subject to that of the Legislative Body." This is a jurisdictional issue: if society as a whole has no right to interfere with religion, neither does the legislature, for its "jurisdiction is both derivative and limited."[217] Madison said the proposed bill was objectionable precisely because it "implies either that the Civil Magistrate is a competent judge of religious truth, or that he may employ religion as an engine of civil policy."[218]

The presentation style may be more reminiscent of a political philosopher like John Locke rather than of a theologian like John Calvin. But underneath the stylistic differences, the ideas Madison presented are right in line with Reformation theology. Essentially, Madison was simply arguing that the state does not have the jurisdiction to meddle in the church's business, because religion is a separate relationship between God and man.[219] The similarity to the Reformation is probably more than coincidental. Madison very likely knew the tradition he was drawing on. In fact, historian George Bancroft suggested that Madison may have been drawing on some of the "theological lore" he had learned in college, where he studied under John Witherspoon.[220]

THE FIRST AMENDMENT

The First Amendment to the U.S. Constitution was all about jurisdiction. The federalists, supporters of the Constitution, did not believe that a bill of rights was necessary or desirable. The basic theory of the Constitution was that the federal government had only the powers delegated to it.[221] Since the federal government had no delegated authority to legislate in regard to religion, there was no need for concern.[222] But states suspicious of the federal government wanted to make doubly sure that there would never be any question about certain things being off-limits for the federal government. Many states ratified the Constitution with the demand that a bill of rights be amended to the Constitution as an additional safeguard against federal usurpation of power. The Bill of Rights was drafted to keep the bargain.[223] Behind the scenes, the non-established religious groups, led by the Baptists, constantly pressed the issue of governmental jurisdiction (or lack thereof) over religion. These are essentially the same forces that defeated the 1784 bill in the Virginia

House of Delegates—and they have a great deal of the responsibility for putting the separation of church and state into the First Amendment.[224]

The resulting products, the religion clauses of the First Amendment, have been the subject of reams of scholarship. For our purposes, it is sufficient to note what the First Amendment did as a theological statement about the institutional relationship between church and state: It prohibited the national civil government as an institution from interfering with the church as an institution.[225] It did nothing to restrain its framers from making public acknowledgments of God. In fact, when the House of Representatives voted to approve the Bill of Rights, Elias Boudinot recommended that the president declare a day of thanksgiving. President Washington willingly complied.[226] There certainly was no separation of God from government.

What was absolutely clear from the beginning was that the First Amendment created a distinction between the institution of the church and the institution of the civil government. The First Amendment *did* prohibit Congress from involving itself in church affairs. It could not enter the jurisdictional sphere of the church.[227] When put in these terms, the First Amendment is a natural fit with the two-jurisdictions approach of the Reformation.[228] Michael McConnell, a distinguished legal scholar and former federal judge, has succinctly stated the case: "The two-kingdoms view of competing authorities is at the heart of our First Amendment."[229]

CHAPTER 5 IN A NUTSHELL...

- Pilgrims and Puritans come to the New World to escape the conflict with King James and King Charles.
- The Puritans recognize church and state as distinct institutions.
- Scottish immigrants bring the legacy of John Knox to America, recognizing distinctions between church and state.
- Church establishments in America—where a particular church

is established by state law—violate the principle of separate institutions.

- The Baptists and other dissenters lead the fight to disestablish state churches.
- The principle that church and state have separate jurisdictions becomes embodied in the First Amendment to the U.S. Constitution.

PART II: THE LAW OF CHURCH AND STATE TODAY

CHAPTER 6: THE LEGAL OUTWORKING: CHURCH DISCIPLINE AND THE CONSTITUTION TODAY

We met Pastor C.L. "Buddy" Westbrook in the introduction to this book. During a personal counseling session, he had learned that church member Peggy Penley was engaging in a "biblically inappropriate" extramarital sexual relationship. [230] Pastor Westbrook began to work through the biblical process for dealing with sin outlined in Matthew 18. Unfortunately, Penley was unresponsive and unrepentant in the face of private confrontation. Pastor Westbrook took the final step in the disciplinary process when he published a letter to the congregation urging church members to break fellowship with Penley for her unrepentant violation of biblical principles. [231] In response, Penley sued Pastor Westbrook in Texas court. [232]

When we first looked at this case at the start of this book, we caught a glimpse of the human side of this legal dispute. But now, with the benefit of historical perspective, we should recognize something new about the case. It was not just about privacy or the duties of counselors or about when to get the church involved in an issue. It was about the relationship between the church and the state. Could a Texas court tell a church that it couldn't follow its own understanding of the Bible? Would the court tell a pastor that the state valued Penley's privacy more highly than it valued the church's religious beliefs—even though Penley had voluntarily joined the church knowing what the church believed about church discipline? Depending on how the court decided the case, the stakes could be high. If a court can tell a church how to run its own affairs, then the state would be above the church.

The case went all the way to the Texas Supreme Court. The nine justices of the court unanimously decided in favor of Pastor Westbrook—and in favor of the historic meaning of the separation of church and state. The court recognized that the autonomy of churches "has long been afforded broad constitutional protection."[233] It went on to explain, "It seems to be settled law in this land of religious liberty that the civil courts have no power or jurisdiction to determine the regularity or validity of the judgment of a church tribunal . . . ."[234]

* * *

The long history of jurisdictional distinctions between church and state in theology lives on in the legal doctrine that the Texas court invoked—church autonomy. The church autonomy doctrine "prohibits civil court review of internal church disputes involving matters of faith, doctrine, church governance, and polity."[235]

With church autonomy doctrine, we come full circle. We began with the challenges churches face when they wish to exercise biblical church discipline. We then saw centuries of struggle to achieve the right balance between church and state, with the exercise of church discipline often taking a central role as the flashpoint of controversy. Finally, we arrived at the First Amendment, set in the context of centuries of theological debate and scholarship. Now with the doctrine of church autonomy, we will see that the First Amendment, even today, provides the very types of protection for the independence of the church that so many throughout church history longed for—and that pastors and churches today need as much as ever.

CHURCH AUTONOMY IN THE FIRST AMENDMENT

Watson v. Jones (1872) was the first church autonomy case to reach the U.S. Supreme Court. The Civil War had divided the people of Kentucky over the issues of slavery and secession. At Walnut Street Presbyterian Church in Louisville, Kentucky, the church body split into proslavery and antislavery factions. In the leadership battle that followed, the Louisville church ignored the orders of the General Assembly of the Presbyterian Church that could have resolved the matter. When the war ended in 1865, the church members took the dispute to court, fighting for control of the church property. When the dispute reached the Supreme Court, the Court emphatically said that this was a matter for the duly-constituted leadership of the Presbyterian Church. It said that the general rule, "founded in a broad and sound view of the relations of church and state under our system of laws," requires that the civil courts must defer to the church authorities whenever "questions of discipline, or of faith, or ecclesiastical rule" were involved.[236]

Eighty years later, the issue of church autonomy reached the Supreme Court again.[237] The New York legislature had passed a law that would have severed the ties between the Russian Orthodox Church in New York and the Russian Orthodox Church's patriarch in Moscow. The Court struck this law down in the case of *Kedroff v. St. Nicholas Cathedral* (1952), explaining that the New York legislature could not set the rules for the church. The Court relied not only on the precedent of the *Watson* decision, but also on the Constitution. When the issue is about the control of church matters, the church must have the final say. The state cannot interfere with the church—and if it tries to, it is violating the First Amendment of the Constitution.

This principle of First Amendment protection for churches was resoundingly reaffirmed in January 2012, when the U.S. Supreme Court decided the case of *Hosanna-Tabor Evangelical Lutheran Church and School v. Equal Employment Opportunity Commission (EEOC).* In this case, a church had fired one of its ministers and the minister, in response, filed a complaint against the church with the EEOC. The question was whether the EEOC could force a church to rehire a minister against its will, and the Supreme Court said no. "Both Religion Clauses [in the First Amendment] bar the government from interfering with the decision of a religious group to fire one of its ministers."[238] This statement is significant, for there are very few cases that are actually based on *both* of the First Amendment's religion clauses.

The first "religion clause" is the "Establishment Clause," which prohibits the government from "establishing" a religion. ("Congress shall make no law respecting an *establishment* of religion ....") The second "religion clause" is the "Free Exercise Clause," which protects the practice of religion. ("Congress shall make no law respecting an establishment of religion, or prohibiting the *free exercise* thereof ....") Usually, the courts decide a case on the basis of one clause or the other, but not both. Church autonomy doctrine is an exception because it brings together both religion clauses in the First Amendment.[239] Civil governmental intrusion into the jurisdiction of church government would entangle that government entity with religion and thereby violate the Establishment Clause. (For instance, when the civil government intrudes into church affairs, it is likely to end up making doctrinal decisions for the church—and this would lead to the state "establishing" a religion.) At the same time, by getting involved in the jurisdiction of church government, the state would infringe on the free exercise of religion by telling a church what it may or may not do.[240]

The legal basis for church autonomy doctrine is as solid as anything gets in the law—grounded in two clauses of the U.S. Constitution. But there's more to it than that. When courts have considered the rationale underlying church autonomy doctrine, they have unwittingly echoed some of the theological principles of "two jurisdictions" that we looked at earlier. Two key points are especially emphasized. First, the courts recognize the governmental nature of the two "spheres," church and state. Second, these two governments are recognized as equals, such that neither is superior or inferior to the other.

TWO GOVERNMENTS

Theologians have long recognized that church and state are separate governments, but Western society has lost sight of this principle in the twentieth century. As the modern state has grown in size and importance, the word "government" has become almost exclusively associated with the *civil* government. But in the church autonomy cases, the courts have countered this trend. Sounding remarkably like the Reformers, they recognize that the state is just one government among others, including church government. As the Texas Supreme Court explained in the *Westbrook* case:

> [T]he First Amendment recognizes two spheres of sovereignty when deciding matters of government and religion. The religion clauses are designed to "prevent, as far as possible, the intrusion of either [religion or government] into the precincts of the other," and are premised on the notion that "both religion and government can best work to achieve their lofty aims if each is left free from the other within its respective sphere."[241]

The state cannot be absolutized as the sole source of real government. Church autonomy doctrine recognizes that there are many spheres of law covering many different governments—just as Abraham Kuyper explained over a century ago.[242] This principle is basic to the judicial treatment of autonomy.

The U.S. Supreme Court made this clear from the very beginning of its church autonomy jurisprudence in *Watson v. Jones* (1872). In *Watson*, the Court said that the foundation for church autonomy is found in the right of the people to create religious associations.[243] Reiterating this point in 1952, the Supreme Court recognized the "power [of churches] to decide for themselves, free from state interference, matters of church government as well as those of faith and doctrine."[244] The Texas court in *Westbrook* repeated this principle, calling this power a "fundamental right."[245]

If, then, there is a right to organize churches as self-governing religious associations, it logically follows that the state must respect this governmental system, as the Supreme Court recognized:

> All who unite themselves to such a body do so with an implied consent to this government, and are bound to submit to it. But it would be a vain consent and would lead to the total subversion of such religious bodies, if any one aggrieved by one of their decisions could appeal to the secular courts and have them reversed. It is of the essence of these religious unions, and of their right to establish tribunals for the decision of questions arising among themselves, that those decisions should be binding in all cases of ecclesiastical cognizance, subject only to such appeals as the organism itself provides for.[246]

John Calvin would have heartily agreed.

EQUAL BUT DISTINCT

Neither of the two spheres is superior to the other. The Reformation thinkers reasoned that since both were ordained by God, neither could claim superiority over the other, and both answer to the same Superior:

> The church—as an institution—does not have authority over the affairs of civil government, and the state—as an institution—does not have authority over the affairs of church government .... Acknowledgment of this separation comes from a recognition that God is the source of all power.[247]

It may be rare for the courts to actually go back and explain the theological rationale, but what they do in practice really does fulfill this theological idea—two governments operating concurrently, with equal authority within their separate spheres.

The courts recognize that the basic issue is jurisdictional. The two governments, church and state, must operate side by side, as it were, because they both operate in different jurisdictions. The U.S. Supreme Court recognized all this in the *Watson* case back in 1872. Because church and state operate in different realms, "the judicial eye cannot penetrate the veil of the church." When people join a church, the court said, they become members upon the conditions set by their churches. "[T]hey thereby submit to the ecclesiastical power and cannot now invoke the supervisory power of the civil tribunals."[248]

Not only did the Supreme Court recognize that it had no right to interfere with the church, it also recognized that there was a risk that even a well-intentioned court would probably make big mistakes if it tried to get involved:

> It is not to be supposed that the judges of the civil courts can be as competent in the ecclesiastical law and religious

> faith of all these bodies as the ablest men in each are in
> reference to their own. It would therefore be an appeal
> from the more learned tribunal in the law which should
> decide the case, to one which is less so.[249]

In other words, even at the pragmatic level of trying to get an issue resolved, the civil courts are ill-equipped to do the job.

The courts have not always articulated the jurisdictional principle consistently. Even though church autonomy is recognized by courts nationwide, and even though the jurisdictional distinction between church and state is built into church autonomy, courts have still found this issue confusing. In a few of the worst cases, some courts lost sight of the basis of autonomy by asking only the pragmatic question—will this court do a better job making this decision than the church would do?—and then (rather presumptuously) answering the question in the affirmative. The jurisdictional issue was forgotten.[250] In two Alabama cases,[251] the state's Supreme Court decided the outcome of contested church elections. The decisions were premised on the notion that the civil judiciary could decide "whether the fundamentals of due process have been observed" in a church proceeding.[252] In a dissenting opinion, the chief justice pointed out that the false implication of these cases was "that the state is merely the less preferred 'power' for determining ecclesiastical and religious matters . . . ." Such is not the case. "On the contrary, the state is simply *without jurisdiction* in such matters: 'It belongs not to the civil power to enter into or review the proceedings of a spiritual court.'"[253]

The chief justice had the better argument here, thanks to the Constitution's protection of the church from state interference. In principle, genuine church government decisions are no more subject to the jurisdiction of the civil courts than the people of Illinois are subject to the jurisdiction of the Alabama courts.

Some state courts recognize not only that the Constitution keeps church matters out of the jurisdiction of the civil courts—they also recognize that this is a jurisdictional defense in a very technical legal sense. Usually, any defenses one has in a lawsuit are waived if they are not raised at the beginning of a court proceeding. (To put it in less technical terms, if you're sued but wait too long to assert a defense, you're out of luck.) But if the court lacks subject matter jurisdiction, that is a defense that can be raised any time. North Carolina's highest court recently made this point. It held that a church can defend itself on grounds of church autonomy at *any point* in the court proceedings. By recognizing that church autonomy can be raised at any time, the North Carolina courts acknowledged that it is a basic issue of subject matter jurisdiction.[254]

On a theoretical level, this approach makes sense, and it reinforces our point about the *jurisdictional* nature of the separation of church and state. Yet a word of caution is in order. Unlike these state courts, the federal courts don't classify church autonomy as a "jurisdictional" defense in the technical sense that would allow you to raise the issue at any time in the lawsuit.[255] This is an anomaly in the otherwise robust framework of church autonomy law. The federal courts recognize that the First Amendment prohibits the government from interfering in the internal workings of churches—in other words, recognizing that the civil government lacks jurisdiction over internal church matters. But at the same time, the federal courts require that church autonomy be raised as a regular defense at the outset of the lawsuit,[256] not a jurisdictional defense that can be brought up anytime. As long as the church (or its lawyer) remembers to raise the defense of church autonomy at the outset of a lawsuit, the church is safe, and this confusing rule won't cause the church any trouble. But it would be a step towards greater theoretical consistency for the federal courts to recognize the church autonomy defense as jurisdictional in the technical sense.

On the whole, though, the state of church autonomy doctrine is encouraging. Most courts across the nation *do* understand the basics of the doctrine. The Supreme Court resoundingly reinforced the basic principles of church autonomy in its 2012 *Hosanna-Tabor* decision. And even the terminology used by the courts seems to be moving in the right direction. The term, "ecclesiastical abstention," is often used interchangeably with "church autonomy."[257] There is no real difference in the way the courts are currently using them,[258] but there are subtle distinctions. "Abstention" could be taken as suggesting that a court is voluntarily staying out of the dispute as an exercise of prudence. "Autonomy," on the other hand, suggests something stronger; it implies that the courts are jurisdictionally incapable of adjudicating an ecclesiastical issue. From the theological perspective, "autonomy" is the more accurate term—and, encouragingly, it is the term getting used most often.[259] The Reformation doctrine of the equality of the two spheres, church and state, remains healthy and well—and indeed, revitalized as the courts have asserted the equality of the "spheres of sovereignty."[260]

CHAPTER 6 IN A NUTSHELL...

- American courts today recognize that churches have a right to run their own affairs.
- The principle that the (civil) government can't interfere with church government is a legal doctrine called "church autonomy."
- Church autonomy is based on the First Amendment to the U.S. Constitution.
- Church autonomy recognizes that:
  - o Both the church and the state are forms of "government."
  - o The church and the state are equals with distinct roles.

CHAPTER 7: WHAT DOES "CHURCH AUTONOMY DOCTRINE" PROTECT?

The central concern of pastors and theologians who advocated a jurisdictional theory of church and state was to preserve the freedom of church government from secular interference. Two of the quintessential church governmental functions are discipline and the election or appointment of officers.

Discipline is unique because it is the occasion where doctrine meets practical reality—it is the only situation where the church uses sanctions.[261] Five hundred years ago, Calvin said that biblical admonitions and discipline in the church would not be possible without a jurisdictional realm for the church—and this is still true today.[262]

Church elections or appointments are similarly important. A church's ability to choose its own leadership goes to the heart of a church's status as an "equal" but distinct government. If the state can intervene or interfere with the church's choice of leadership and governance, then the church would be *under* the state, not *separate* from it.

These two church governmental functions are at the core of church autonomy protections. Church autonomy issues also arise in church property disputes. These usually arise when there is a split in the membership of a church, making it difficult to determine which of several factions is in fact the rightful church government with a right to the property. Confusion and divergent opinions have surrounded the resolution of church property disputes. The real heart of church autonomy, however, is not the property cases (which are often deeply entangled with technical legal issues relating to property title, trusts, and the like). At the heart of church autonomy protection are the practical functions of church government—discipline and the election or appointment of church officers. In these situations, the church is always protected. Let's take a closer look.

CHURCH DISCIPLINE

The power of a church to exercise discipline over its members is a universally recognized Christian doctrine.[263] As Calvin explained, "[S]o . . . that doctrine may not be held in derision, those who profess to be of the household of faith ought to be judged according to the doctrine which is taught."[264] This is done "not . . . by fine, imprisonment, or other civil penalties," but "by the word of God only. For the severest punishment of the Church . . . is excommunication . . . ."[265]

Civil suits have often come into the courts based on the church's execution of discipline. And with very few exceptions, the courts have held that these suits were outside of their jurisdiction. As one old case stated, "The [disciplinary] proceedings of the church are quasi judicial, and therefore those who complain, or give testimony, or act and vote, or pronounce the result, . . . acting in good faith, and within the scope of the authority conferred by this limited jurisdiction, . . . are protected by law."[266]

An outstanding recent example is the case we have already highlighted, *Westbrook v. Penley*. When Penley sued Pastor Westbrook for initiating church disciplinary proceedings, Westbrook was protected by the constitutional principles of church autonomy.[267] In its opinion, the Texas Supreme Court wrote, "[T]he right of a church to decide for itself whom it may admit into fellowship or who shall be expelled or excluded from its fold cannot be questioned by the courts, when no civil or property rights are involved."[268] The *Westbrook* court is squarely in line here with the most recent Supreme Court precedent in regard to church disciplinary action.

In a 1976 case,[269] the Serbian Orthodox Church had initiated an investigation on the controversial American bishop Dionisije Milivojevich. Milivojevich was suspended from his responsibilities and ultimately defrocked as a result of the investigation. The hierarchal church leadership in Yugoslavia also ordered a reorganization of the diocese. Milivojevich sued the diocese, trying to get a judicial declaration that he was the true bishop of the diocese and a court order to prevent church officials from interfering with the assets of his diocese. The Supreme Court ruled against Milivojevich. It explained that the court should not get involved in a church governmental decision, which is protected by the church autonomy doctrine of the First Amendment:

> [W]here resolution of the disputes cannot be made without extensive inquiry by civil courts into religious law and polity, the First and Fourteenth Amendments mandate that civil courts shall not disturb the decisions of the highest ecclesiastical tribunal within a church of hierarchical polity, but must accept such decisions as binding on them, in their application to the religious issues of doctrine or polity before them.[270]

The *Milivojevich* decision was followed three years later by *Jones v. Wolf*. Some legal commentators thought that the *Jones* case was a change of position by the Supreme Court, giving less autonomy protection to churches.[271] Actually, the *Jones* case simply dealt with a different issue that did not raise the same church autonomy concerns. The two approaches are not nearly as different as they may appear at first glance.[272]

Jones was a property dispute of the classic "church split" variety. In

Jones, the Supreme Court said that the church government was only incidentally involved in the determination of who owned the church property. As a result, the Court held that the courts *could* decide who owned the church property. The key point is that resolving the church property dispute did not force the Court to step in and make a church government decision. Rather, the Court simply had to apply standard legal principles (such as how to construe a deed to property).

But the court made it clear that if the situation were otherwise, the only proper authority to adjudicate the matter would be the church government: "If in such a case the interpretation of the instruments of ownership would require the civil court to resolve a religious controversy, then the court must defer to the resolution of the doctrinal issue by the authoritative ecclesiastical body." [273]

This is very different from the situation in *Milivojevich*, where the basic issue was the church's ability to discipline a member of its authority structure. In *Jones*, the court just had to apply standard legal rules of deeds and trusts to determine ownership of property. In *Milivojevich*, the court never suggested that it could apply the internal rules of the Serbian Orthodox Church to determine if the church had properly followed its own rules to divide a diocese. Where *Milivojevich* emphasized the jurisdictional inability of courts to "pierce the veil"[274] of church government,[275] *Jones* emphasized the ability of courts to decide cases by the application of "neutral principles."[276]

The point is that the rationale for deference to church government discipline decisions, as presented in *Milivojevich*, remained intact even after *Jones*. Discipline is doctrinal; as Calvin explained, "[T]hose who profess to be of the household of faith ought to be judged according to the doctrine which is taught."[277] There is no way to resolve an issue of church discipline by "neutral principles" of law.

The overwhelming majority of court decisions have recognized this fact.[278] Church autonomy considerations raised by church discipline actions were held to bar a multitude of suits against the church. Disgruntled parishioners have been creative in the kinds of lawsuits they bring. Sometimes they say that church discipline has "defamed" them,[279] or has inflicted "emotional distress" on them;[280] sometimes they claim that a church hierarchy has been negligent in supervising a pastor.[281] In these and other cases,[282] church autonomy will be a good defense as long as theological and doctrinal issues were the real decision-makers.

The courts have recognized a related doctrine, known as the "ministerial exception," which is applied in discrimination claims arising out of church hiring and firing decisions.[283] (We'll have more to say on this in a moment when we turn our attention to church decision-making.) In addition, Illinois[284] and Pennsylvania[285] cases have held that the protection of church autonomy doctrine extends to protect religious educational institutions (church schools and colleges).

As the *Westbrook* court noted, "the autonomy of a church in managing its affairs and deciding matters of 'church discipline . . . or the conformity of the members of the church to the standard of morals required of them' has long been afforded broad constitutional protection."[286] And well established it seems to be.

In 1875, three years after the *Watson* decision, Associate Justice of the Supreme Court William Strong, a Presbyterian, gave two lectures at Union Theological Seminary in New York on the nature of church-state relations. He stated:

> Again, the law recognizes the right of every church to
> determine finally who are, and who are not its members.
> Herein is a marked difference between churches and
> other organizations. . . . But a church is allowed to
> determine for itself, construing its own organic rules,
> whether a member has been cut off; and no civil court
> will inquire whether the motion was regularly made, or

issue a mandamus to compel a restoration. It accepts the decisions of church courts upon questions of membership as not subject to civil law review.[287]

In other words, the civil government is to respect and defend the jurisdiction of the church to exercise its own discipline. The attitude of the courts toward discipline is about as on-point as it gets for making a legal reality of the Reformers' ideal—the "spiritual power . . . altogether distinct from the power of the sword."[288]

CHURCH DECISION-MAKING

The ability of a church to follow its own church government (polity) for making decisions without a civil court telling it whether it did so rightly is a basic practical outworking of "two jurisdictions" theology. This is an issue that is distinct from discipline. Discipline issues are about the ability of a church to stick by a decision it has made; polity decision-making is about the ability to make the decisions in the first place without a court telling the church how to do so. These distinct issues do have some overlap and have arisen in the same case.

Again, the courts have echoed the sentiments of the Reformers. The Supreme Court first articulated the right to manage church administration in its *Watson* decision in 1872:

> [W]henever the questions of discipline, or of faith, or ecclesiastical rule, custom, or law have been decided by the highest of these church judicatories to which the matter has been carried, the legal tribunals must accept such decisions as final, and as binding on them, in their application to the case before them.[289]

Over fifty years later, the Court had to confront the issue again in an unusual case involving an endowed position as a chaplain. A parishioner had willed her property to the church back in 1820 and provided that the position of chaplain should be held by her nearest living male relative. But the chaplain had to be properly approved by the Roman Catholic authorities. Everything went fine for several generations, until Raul Gonzalez was presented to take over the chaplaincy in 1922. The archbishop refused to appoint him, saying that Raul wasn't qualified: Raul was only ten years old, and besides that, he had not taken any theology classes! A lawsuit was filed to secure the position for Raul. But the Supreme Court held that the civil courts could not intermeddle with the appointment of a chaplain in the Catholic Church. Doing so would interfere with the self-government of the church:

> Because the appointment is a canonical act, it is the
> function of the church authorities to determine what
> the essential qualifications of a chaplain are and whether
> the candidate possesses them. . . . [T]he decisions of the
> proper church tribunals on matters purely ecclesiastical
> . . . are accepted in litigation before the secular courts as
> conclusive, because the parties in interest made them so
> by contract or otherwise.[290]

As mentioned in chapter 6, in the 1950s, the Supreme Court had to deal with a New York statute that transferred the property of the Russian Orthodox Church to an American church body. The idea was to take all power away from the church hierarchy in Soviet Moscow. But the Supreme Court invalidated this law as an inappropriate attempt by the civil government to interfere with church government issues. They invoked the old *Watson* decision and made the point even stronger: "The [*Watson*] opinion radiates . . . a spirit of freedom for religious organizations, an independence from secular control or manipulation—in short, power to decide for themselves, free from state interference, matters of church government as well as those of faith and doctrine."[291]

A classic example of a polity decision outside the cognizance of the civil courts occurred in a recent New Jersey case. The church's governing body terminated the pastor over a doctrinal dispute, and the pastor refused to leave. When the controversy went to the courts, the trial court appointed a moderator to "supervise and oversee the annual meeting election, and to resolve issues of church membership, voter qualification, election notice, and voting procedures."[292] This, the appellate court held, was clearly unconstitutional, and it reversed the lower court's decision. The appellate court noted that "the intrachurch dispute here is the type of primarily religious dispute that led to complete judicial deference in *Watson v. Jones . . . .*"[293]

In a similar (and even more recent) determination, the North Carolina Supreme Court was explicit in recognizing that a "church's view of the role of the pastor, staff, and church leaders, their authority and compensation, and church management" are affected by the "church's religious doctrine." As a result, the court concluded, the "courts must defer to the church's internal governing body" on such matters.[294]

In pure church government decisions, more than in discipline cases, there are serious problems for the courts to grapple with. For example, when a church membership splits, and it is not clear which part of the membership is the rightful owner of church property, the outcome may appear to turn on which side has kept proper church procedures in voting for or against the division, or which side stuck to the church's original doctrine. But the courts have not gone this route. It would be a doctrinal determination, inappropriate for a court, to resolve such an issue by construing the church's beliefs and polity. This was the message of the Supreme Court's decision in the case of *Presbyterian Church v. Hull Church* (1969). That case involved a church property dispute; a church had split off from its denominational affiliation, and in order to determine who got the property, the court would have had to decide whether the original church denomination had "abandoned or departed from" its

original doctrine. This was a determination outsia.
courts, the Supreme Court held.[295]

Not all courts have been as conscious of the need to
church autonomy in these settings—in a pair of cases, an A
court was so bold as to decide church elections outright. But
the exceptions. In general, here as elsewhere in the autonomy fie.
courts have honored the principle of two jurisdictions.

A final group of cases relating to church leadership are known as
the "ministerial exception" cases. The "ministerial exception" is really
just a name for applying the church autonomy principle in the context
of employment law. Federal law prohibits a variety of forms of employment discrimination. Some of these laws would cause serious problems
if they were applied to churches.

For instance, if churches could be sued for discriminating on the
basis of gender, then any church that believed (for example) in male
leadership for the church could end up in court for not hiring a woman
as pastor.

Or, in a real-life case, a church found out that its full-time youth
minister had had a civil commitment ceremony with a same-sex
partner.[296] The church leadership fired the youth minister for entering into an unbiblical same-sex partnership. The minister sued under
the federal employment laws, arguing that this was a form of sexual
harassment.

If the courts ruled against the church in either of these examples,
then the federal government would be telling the church that it
couldn't follow its own understanding of the Bible. The courts have
recognized that this is a matter of basic religious freedom and that
the First Amendment's principle of church autonomy requires that
churches and other religious organizations get an exception from these
antidiscrimination laws. The courts have called this the "ministerial
exception."

.e ministerial exception recently came before the U.S. Supreme
 in the *Hosanna-Tabor* case. In *Hosanna-Tabor*, the Court emphati-
 reaffirmed the ministerial exception and the principle of church
.onomy. It recognized:

> Requiring a church to accept or retain an unwanted min-
> ister, or punishing a church for failing to do so, intrudes
> upon more than a mere employment decision. Such ac-
> tion interferes with the internal governance of the church,
> depriving the church of control over the selection of those
> who will personify its beliefs.[297]

The First Amendment once again protected churches. And the
Supreme Court recognized that "the authority to select and control who
will minister to the faithful—a matter 'strictly ecclesiastical'—is the
church's alone."[298]

CHAPTER 7 IN A NUTSHELL...

- The church autonomy doctrine protects churches that exercise
  church discipline from being sued.
- The church autonomy doctrine prevents courts from trying to
  get involved in decisions that belong to the church government,
  including:
  - o Selecting leaders
  - o Hiring and firing employees.

CHAPTER 8: THE LIMITS OF AUTONOMY: ANSWERING THE COMMON OBJECTION TO CHURCH AUTONOMY

Whenever the subject of church autonomy comes up, it seems that someone usually objects, "Wait! That will allow churches to get away with anything, even crime!"

Recently, especially since 2002, the Roman Catholic Church has been rocked by a series of sexual molestation scandals. In the spring of 2010, *Newsweek* published an essay by Christopher Hitchens with the provocative title, "Bring the Pope to Justice." In this piece, Hitchens argued that the pope should be personally held liable for the scandals. "Mentally remove his papal vestments and imagine him in a suit, and Joseph Ratzinger becomes just a Bavarian bureaucrat who has failed in the only task he was ever set—that of damage control."[299] Respected human rights advocate Geoffrey Robertson agreed that the pope could be facing some liability. Whatever one thinks of Hitchens' specific allegations, no one can deny that the issues he raised pose a challenge to the church. Tragically, we know that abuse *does* happen even in Christian churches. And this poses a dilemma. Can we protect religious freedom and church autonomy without somehow protecting criminal conduct? Do we really want church autonomy protections for churches that might commit criminal abuses?

The fact is, autonomy does not allow churches to get away with crime. The problem of church abuses is not something new in the twenty-first century. Over several centuries, theologians and legal scholars alike have confronted the issue. And what is particularly fascinating is the fact that even here, at the limits of church autonomy, much of the legal theory follows the insights of Reformation theology.

BECKET, THE REFORMATION, AND THE "BENEFIT OF CLERGY"

During the Middle Ages, with the medieval church at the zenith of its authority, the church claimed an almost complete immunity from the jurisdiction of the civil courts.[300] This included exclusive ecclesiastical jurisdiction over "all civil and criminal cases involving clerics."[301] In other words, the civil government could not punish a clergyman who committed a crime. Only the church itself could punish these criminal clergymen. In England, this exemption that the church had from felony prosecution or suit was known as "benefit of clergy."[302]

The broad protections of the benefit of clergy frustrated kings for several centuries, and many attempts were made to circumscribe it, with varying degrees of success.[303] This was actually the issue that precipitated the showdown between King Henry II and Thomas Becket that we discussed in chapter 2.

The friction between Henry and Becket was centered on the king's ability to prosecute clergymen for felonies.[304] It was reported to Henry that clergymen were responsible for hundreds of murders that were going unpunished because of their protected status as clergymen.[305] Henry recognized that this had to be stopped. When he convened the council at Clarendon, this was the primary matter of concern. The Constitutions of Clarendon said that, "Clergymen charged and accused of anything shall, on being summoned by a justice of the king, come into his court to be responsible there for whatever it may seem to the king's court they should there be responsible for . . . ."[306] This was the clause that most offended

Becket. After the uproar in the wake of Becket's assassination, Henry was forced to abrogate the offending portions of the Constitutions of Clarendon—a victory for the ecclesiastical courts.[307]

Given this long history of tension and frustration with the clergy's extensive exemption from criminal prosecution, it is not surprising that the reformers specifically criticized the abuses of the ecclesiastical courts. Calvin wrote:

> Whoredom, lasciviousness, drunkenness, and similar
> iniquities, they not only tolerate, but by a kind of tacit ap-
> probation encourage and confirm, and that not among the
> people only, but also among the clergy. Out of many they
> summon a few, either that they may not seem to wink too
> strongly, or that they may mulct them in money. I say
> nothing of the plunder, rapine, peculation, and sacrilege,
> which are there committed. I say nothing of the kind
> of persons who are for the most part appointed to the
> office. It is enough, and more than enough, that when
> the Romanists boast of their spiritual jurisdiction, we are
> ready to show that nothing is more contrary to the proce-
> dure instituted by Christ, that it has no more resemblance
> to ancient practice than darkness has to light.[308]

The upheaval and drastic alterations to church authority occurring during the Reformation era made it the ideal time to constrict the canon law sphere of ecclesiastical courts. This constriction is precisely what happened—yet without abolishing ecclesiastical jurisdiction altogether.[309]

The eighteenth century legal scholar, Sir William Blackstone, sum-marized the effect of the Reformation era in his influential *Commentaries on the Laws of England*. He noted both the continued recognition of a sphere of ecclesiastical immunity, and the fact that it had been constricted from its former scope: "[The clergy] have ... large privileges allowed them by our municipal law: and had formerly much greater, which were abridged at the time of the reformation on account of the ill use which the popish clergy had endeavoured to make of them."[310]

This restriction of ecclesiastical jurisdiction fit with the social and political trends set in motion by the Reformation. But it also fit with the Reformation's theology. The Reformers recognized that the church and the state were to be institutionally separated, and yet were not intended to be at odds with each other. There was to be no dichotomy between the church and the state.[311] But the old form of ecclesiastical courts, which exempted clergy from the cognizance of the civil courts, put the church and the state at odds. The state could not protect its citizens, and the clergy were not accountable to the same standards as the citizens. When clergy and laity were to be tried in different judicial systems, the effect could only be dichotomization. The Reformers did not see this as the command of Scripture, nor as the example of history. Calvin wrote:

> To [the Catholic Church's ecclesiastical] jurisdiction is
> annexed the immunity claimed by the Romish clergy.
> They deem it unworthy of them to answer before a civil
> judge in personal causes; and consider both the liberty
> and dignity of the church to consist in exemption from
> ordinary tribunals and laws.[312]

The bishops in the early church had a better understanding of this issue, Calvin wrote. They "did not think it any injury to themselves and their order to act as subjects"[313]—that is, they recognized that the civil government had jurisdiction even over the clergy when it came to civil matters.

In contrast to the clergy-laity distinction stood the Reformation's doctrine of the priesthood of all believers.[314] All believers were recognized as "priests and kings" before God. The priesthood of the believer meant that all of Christendom would (ideally) be comprised of "churchmen" in a new sense of the word.[315] To exempt them all from prosecution for crimes would be to destroy civil order and would indeed destroy the institution of the state. This couldn't be right, since the state was itself ordained by God.

The Reformation did not deny the Catholic position that the church retains jurisdiction over ecclesiastical issues and the state over civil issues—this it affirmed. What the Reformation did was to try to classify the offence to the proper jurisdiction based upon the nature of the offence rather than by the status of the offender.[316] Thus, the Puritans' legal code in Massachusetts would provide, "Civill Authoritie hath power and libertie to deale with any Church member in a way of Civill Justice, notwithstanding any Church relation, office or interest."[317]

For instance, if there was an allegation of theft, the question under the old system of ecclesiastical courts was whether the accused was a clergyman or a layman. A layman could be prosecuted in criminal court, but a clergyman could not. But the proper question is whether this offense is one recognized by the criminal law. If it is, then the offender can be tried in a criminal court. His status as a clergyman or layman does not make any difference.

TODAY: CIVIL JURISDICTION OVER CIVIL OFFENSES

Against this backdrop, courts have refused to recognize claims of autonomy proffered to escape civil or criminal liability for such offenses as sexual assault and molestation. In the Supreme Court's 1872 decision in *Watson v. Jones*, the Court explained that certain crimes were suitable for the civil courts alone to punish:

> There is, perhaps, no word in legal terminology so frequently used as the word jurisdiction, so capable of use in a general and vague sense, and which is used so often by men learned in the law without a due regard to precision

in its application. As regards its use in the matters we
have been discussing it may very well be conceded that if
the General Assembly of the Presbyterian Church should
undertake to try one of its members for murder, and punish him with death or imprisonment, its sentence would
be of no validity in a civil court or anywhere else. Or if
it should at the instance of one of its members entertain
jurisdiction as between him and another member as to
their individual right to property, real or personal, the
right in no sense depending on ecclesiastical questions, its
decision would be utterly disregarded by any civil court
where it might be set up. And it might be said in a certain
general sense very justly, that it was because the General
Assembly had no jurisdiction of the case.[318]

In drawing the line between church and state, the courts have echoed
the concerns of the Reformers. First, the civil jurisdiction should remain
intact over real violations of the civil law. Second, the church's liberties
should be preserved inviolate, including the ability to conduct its own
internal affairs. It has become standard operating procedure for courts to
begin with the "threshold inquiry" of whether the allegedly illegal conduct was "rooted in religious belief."[319] Where it is a matter of doctrine,
the courts keep their hands off. Since the courts have recognized that
matters of "discipline, . . . internal organization, or ecclesiastical rule, custom, or law"[320] are essentially doctrinal, these are protected. On the other
hand, where there is no claim of doctrine at issue, the courts address
this as a civil issue within the judiciary's domain. In so doing, the courts
have embraced, rather than rejected, the Reformation heritage on church
autonomy.

An excellent example of this kind of distinction in practice is a
Rhode Island Superior Court decision on a claim against a church based
on an alleged act of molestation by a priest.[321] In this case, the court

distinguished two different issues. One is whether the priest could be held responsible; the answer was, of course. The second issue was whether the church should also be held responsible for failing to adequately supervise the priest. On this issue, the court said no. Such an inquiry was barred by the autonomy doctrine, because to determine whether the diocese was negligent would require inquiry into the church's manner of employing the priest. In order to make a ruling on this issue, the court would have to decide what a "reasonable" church would do to supervise a priest, and this would require an examination of "the rules, policies and doctrine of the Roman Catholic Church."[322] Because of this doctrinal element, the court recognized that this "examination . . . is prohibited by the First Amendment."[323]

In other words, when the only way the court can determine that a civil wrong was committed is by making a doctrinal determination, the court does not have jurisdiction. At the same time, claims for *intentional* failure to supervise were not barred, because this is within the court's "common law jurisdiction" to protect citizens.[324] And of course, if the lawsuit had been against the priest himself, the priest could not claim the protection of church autonomy doctrine—the court does not need to inquire into any church doctrines to figure out whether he behaved wrongfully.

UNRESOLVED ISSUES

A critical observer might note that underlying this approach to autonomy issues is an unacknowledged assumption that civil morality will not conflict with a religious doctrine. It is easy for the courts to rebut a claim of ecclesiastical immunity by saying, "Sexual molestation is not a doctrine of Church *X*," and proceed to take jurisdiction of the case. But if some exotic religion showed up and explicitly declared that molestation is a doctrine of their organization and subject to its ecclesiastical courts, what then? The conduct would be rooted in religious belief, meeting the "threshold inquiry" to trigger autonomy protections. But no court would let the offender off on a church autonomy theory.[325]

The fact that this has not become an issue (yet) indicates that the church autonomy doctrine has been mostly applied in a culture where the church understands its responsibilities. There are two points to note here. First, the morality of the American legal system is in general accord with biblical morality, and in practice, ecclesiastical disputes have arisen almost exclusively in the Christian context. As a result, the issue of conduct "rooted in religious belief" which is yet clearly a civil crime (ritual torture, for instance) has never arisen. As our culture becomes increasingly pluralistic, however, the issues are likely to become more complicated. Ultimately, the courts will have to confront the difficult question of how to apply a legal system built on two thousand years of Christian western civilization to the panoply of religions and religious institutions that are now in the United States. At the moment, the courts are still dealing primarily with religions in the Western Christian tradition, and the really tricky issues have yet to be dealt with.

Second, the general ecumenical agreement that the power of the "sword" is assigned to civil government, not the church, has meant that churches have never claimed the power to punish violations of biblical morality with civil sanctions. As Calvin wrote:

> [T]he church has not the right of the sword to punish or restrain, has no power to coerce, no prison nor other punishments which the magistrate is wont to inflict... [T]he church [does not] assume anything to herself which is proper to the magistrate, nor is the magistrate competent to what is done by the Church.[326]

It may be the church's duty to use church discipline, including excommunication, to bring a criminal who has already been punished by the civil authorities to repentance.[327] But the courts have never needed to fear churches trying to take control of felonies and similar serious offenses away from the civil authority. (This is all the more reason that churches need to be aware of the limits of their proper role in church discipline, a subject we'll look at in the next chapter.)

Difficult questions will likely arise as other religious traditions without a clear distinction between civil and ecclesiastical law end up in American courts. In the meantime, the fact that Christian theology has made the courts' current job simpler demonstrates as much as anything else the intimate connection between theology and the legal doctrine of autonomy.

GETTING THE ISSUES RIGHT

The decision to apply civil law despite a claim of church autonomy is rarely clear-cut. Still, most of the cases where this has happened[328] appear to fit tolerably within the Reformation paradigm: the courts take jurisdiction over civil issues, unless an alleged civil offense relies on a doctrinal determination to prove its existence.[329] For example:

- A church could not claim church autonomy protection to avoid disclosing information when subpoenaed in a criminal case.[330]

- A church could not claim church autonomy protection to avoid paying unemployment benefits[331] (because this is a secular law of general applicability that did not contradict church government roles).

- When a church was sued for sexual harassment under the federal anti-discrimination law (Title VII[332]), the church could not claim "church autonomy" protection. This was a matter of general civil duties, not a matter for church government decisions.[333]

- When teachers at a church school tried to unionize, the administrators claimed a privilege to not deal with the union on church autonomy grounds. The court said that this was not an appropriate invocation of church autonomy protections.[334]

The classic subject matter in this gray area of the boundaries of church and civil jurisdiction is church property disputes. For legal scholars, there are many very interesting and often complicated issues raised in church property disputes about when church autonomy considerations arise and when it is sufficient to simply consult "neutral" legal principles of property law, contracts, and trusts. In other words, the question is whether this can be resolved by just applying the law of civil government. If so, and it does not involve the courts making church government decisions, then the courts can decide the issue. As the Supreme Court has said, the courts can adjudicate the dispute under legal principles of general applicability, "so long as it involves no consideration of doctrinal matters."[335] This approach remains consistent with the autonomy of church governmental functions: it recognizes that churches do have a legitimate sphere of government where the civil courts cannot infringe.

We should no more expect easy distinctions on the borderlines of church-state jurisdiction than we would in other difficult legal questions, such as those regarding federalism or the separation of powers in the federal government. Two simultaneously operating legal systems inevitably lead to difficult questions about the proper bounds of their authority. In the difficult decisions of where to draw the lines, it is important to remember that the line-drawing act itself is part of our theological heritage.

CHAPTER 8 IN A NUTSHELL...

- Church autonomy doctrine does *not* protect churches or church leaders who commit crimes.
- Crimes are part of the *civil* government's jurisdiction.

PART III: A PRIMER ON KEEPING YOUR CHURCH OUT OF COURT

CHAPTER 9. THE CHURCH AS A GOVERNMENT: CHURCH DISCIPLINE IN THE BIBLE

Church discipline has occupied center stage for most of this book as the flashpoint of controversy between church and state. But if we don't understand what church discipline is really about, we'll misunderstand the history and the law. So now we need to take a close look at church discipline. This will help to flesh out the law and history we've been looking at up to now. Understanding the basics of church discipline is also crucial for church leaders who want to wisely lead a church—and stay out of court. Finally, critics of church autonomy sometimes assume the worst about the church discipline process. When it is badly done, the church discipline process can turn ugly and become easy to caricature.[336] By obtaining a biblical and historical understanding of church discipline, we can get past these misconceptions.[337]

JESUS ON CHURCH DISCIPLINE

The power of the church to exercise discipline is grounded in several biblical passages. The first is in Matthew 16. Peter had just given his great confession of Jesus as the Messiah. Jesus responded that on this rock He would build His church (Matthew 16:18). Jesus then promised authority to this church, His *ecclesia*[338]: "And I will give unto thee the keys of the kingdom of heaven: and whatsoever thou shalt bind on earth shall be bound in heaven: and whatsoever thou shalt loose on earth shall be loosed in heaven."[339]

The terms "binding" and "loosing" were well understood in early Judaism.[340] They referred to the power of the Sanhedrin to give out judicial sentences. What Jesus was saying, then, was that His church had the power to give judicial sentences, too. The judicial structure of first-century Judaism was to be implemented in the body of Messiah. Christians throughout church history have viewed this Scripture as a mandate for the church to exercise discipline, as we shall see. Church discipline has often been called "the power of the keys," in reference to this passage of scripture.

The church might well be empowered to exercise the "power of the keys," but Scripture did not leave churches free to exercise this power in any manner that they saw fit. Scripture lays out procedures for church discipline. The biblical teaching can be best understood when we look at it as establishing two distinct procedures: one for private, personal sins, and another for public, open, and notorious sins. For the former, we turn to Christ's exposition in Matthew 18. For the latter, we look at several epistles by Paul, most especially his first epistle to the Corinthians.

PROCEDURE FOR CHURCH DISCIPLINE: DEALING WITH PRIVATE SINS

Christ explained how we are to deal with private and interpersonal sins. His detailed description of disciplinary procedure comes just two chapters after his original discussion of the power of the keys in Matthew's gospel, and it repeats this same phrase about binding and loosing.

In this passage (Matthew 18), Jesus describes a series of steps for dealing with sins and solving conflicts. Jesus's procedure can apply to many different types of conflicts. He indicated that these principles are especially important for churches by repeating the phrase, "binding and loosing," in this same passage (Matthew 18:18). As we have already seen, "binding and loosing" was understood as a congregational judicial function.

When someone has been wronged, the first step is to personally and privately confront an offender: "Moreover if thy brother shall trespass against thee, go and tell him his fault between thee and him alone: if he shall hear thee, thou hast gained thy brother." (Matthew 18:15) A private resolution is ideal—it best preserves relationships while rectifying whatever problems had come up. Most often, church leadership isn't even involved at this step.

However, if a private resolution cannot be worked out, then a second step is to approach the sinning person with one or two additional parties as witnesses: "But if he will not hear thee, then take with thee one or two more, that in the mouth of two or three witnesses every word may be established" (v. 16). Jesus is quoting here from Deuteronomy 17:6, a passage that requires "two or three" witnesses to establish guilt. In other words, the presence of witnesses acts as a safeguard for all the parties, to ensure that due process is followed. Often, this would be the stage where the additional party could be in church leadership.

If the second approach does not resolve the matter, a third step is to take the matter before the entire congregation: "And if he shall neglect to hear them, tell it unto the church" (v. 17). This gives the offender a final chance to repent and make things right. If someone is in sin, getting the whole congregation involved might be what it takes to get his attention. It's important to note that, at each stage of the discipline process, the goal is repentance and restoration, not punishment for the sake of punishment.

Only if this still does not lead to repentance is the church authorized to take the final and most severe step—treating the unrepentant individual as an unbeliever. In the words of Jesus, "[I]f he neglect to hear the church, let him be unto thee as an heathen man and a publican" (v. 17).

In concluding, Jesus repeats the principle of binding and loosing (Matthew 18:18). This reinforces the principle that the most severe sentence of excommunication—viewing the offender as an unbeliever—is to be issued by the church leaders.[341]

THE DIFFERENCE BETWEEN PUBLIC AND PRIVATE SINS

Matthew 18 is fairly well known as a procedure for correcting sin. But are all situations supposed to be treated the same? What if someone in the church is openly and publicly in sin? What about when that public sin affects the whole church? Is there still a requirement that there be a completely private meeting before any public actions are done in the congregation? As we shall see from Paul's epistles, a more public correction can take place when the sin is public—such as open and notorious scandal or public propagation of false doctrine. Certainly, wisdom might counsel private confrontation as a first step even in some cases where there is a public sin. But such private confrontation is not *required*.

A few examples illustrate the differences between a "private" and a "public" sin:

- Jim is a church member involved in an adulterous relationship. He has kept this a well-guarded secret. His wife confronts him about his unfaithfulness, but Jim ignores her. At this point, it would be appropriate to get the church elders involved. Hopefully, Jim will then take the issue seriously, repent, and start the path to restoring his marriage.

- Joe is a church member involved in an adulterous relationship, but unlike Jim, Joe doesn't attempt to keep it low key. He abandons his wife and children, saying he made a mistake marrying her in the first place, and openly brags about his new girlfriend. Due to Joe's own actions

everyone at church knows about it. In this situation, the
church leadership can take decisive public action, along
the lines that Paul set out in First Corinthians, letting
the entire congregation know that Joe's conduct is wrong.
The goal is to hopefully cause Joe to take the matter seriously, repent, and begin the restoration process.

Public sin "opens the door" to public rebuke. A similar concept
operates in American courts. The law prohibits prosecutors from using
"character evidence"—for instance, evidence Dan the defendant was
dishonest on some prior occasion in order to prove that Dan was a dishonest crook in this particular case. In other words, we aren't supposed to
prosecute people on the theory of "once a crook, always a crook." But if
the defendant tries to defend himself by introducing character evidence
himself—showing that he has a reputation for honesty, for example—then
the defendant has "opened the door" for the prosecutor to fight back by
presenting evidence of bad character. What he couldn't do before, he
can do now. Likewise, in the church situation, people who sin privately
should not have their sins revealed to the whole congregation: the elders
can confront them privately and give them a chance to repent and correct
whatever needs dealt with. But once you've gone public with your sin, you
have opened the door. You can't object to a public correction by the elders.

THE BIBLICAL ANALYSIS OF PUBLIC SINS

The apostle Paul addresses church discipline for public sins most
extensively in his epistles to the Corinthians. The specific problem in
the Corinthian church was sexual immorality or fornication. This was
a public sin in this case because the fornication was flaunted in front of
the congregation: "It is actually reported that there is sexual immorality
among you, and of a kind that is not tolerated even among pagans, for a
man has his father's wife." (1 Corinthians 5:1, ESV). Paul instructs the
Corinthian church to disassociate from those professing faith but living

in sin (1 Corinthians 5:9–11). Specifically, he tells the church to exercise the disciplinary action of excommunication against the church member engaged in fornication (1 Corinthians 5:1–6). The public excommunication was to be done without going through a private process for rebuke and admonition first.

Paul also taught about public discipline in his ministerial instructions to Timothy. "As for those who persist in sin, rebuke them in the presence of all, so that the rest may stand in fear" (1 Timothy 5:20, ESV). Timothy was dealing with heretical teachers, and later in the same epistle, Paul instructed Timothy to withdraw himself from those who teach contrary to the gospel, "consent not to wholesome words," and oppose the "doctrine which is according to godliness" (1 Timothy 6:3). Since teaching is a public function, a public rebuke and disfellowshipping was an appropriate response to heretical teaching. In this case, we see another purpose of discipline (in addition to repentance and restoration)—protecting the congregation. In some situations, repentance might be unlikely but discipline in the form of rebuke would help to protect the congregation from false teaching.

LEVELS OF DISCIPLINE

Excommunication is the most severe sanction that the church can bring. But Paul's epistles demonstrate that there are many options, less severe than excommunication, that allow churches to appropriately and proportionately deal with a situation.

In his first epistle to the church in Thessalonica, Paul instructed the church to "warn them that are unruly" (1 Thessalonians 5:14). But the church was still having problems at the time that Paul wrote his second epistle. Then Paul speaks about those who are "disorderly," a term with stronger negative moral connotations than "unruly" (2 Thessalonians 3:6–15). Paul recommends sterner measures, instructing the believers of Thessalonica "that ye withdraw yourselves from every brother that walketh disorderly" (2 Thessalonians 3:6). He added that, if anyone disregarded the rebukes, they should "note that man, and have no company with him that he may be ashamed" (v. 14). Still, Paul instructed the church, "Do not regard him as an enemy, but warn him as a brother" (2 Thessalonians 3:15, ESV). Since the offender was still to be treated as a brother, this was a less severe form of discipline than full excommunication.[342]

This teaching from Paul shows that there are different levels of discipline. A rebuke, as in 1 Thessalonians, is a form of discipline, but a milder one than disfellowship and excommunication. Indeed, in Titus, Paul explains that rebuke is itself a form of discipline (Titus 1:9–13). (In this passage, the reason for the rebuke is given as well: "that they may be sound in faith.")

Likewise, it would be possible to bar a church member from partaking of the Lord's Table until a sin issue is resolved without disfellowshipping that individual. Again, this is a less severe sanction than full excommunication. Preserving the sanctity of the Lord's Table is necessary. Discipline to preserve its sanctity can be done without going as far as excommunication. While Paul teaches that there are some errant brothers who are to be admonished as brothers (2 Thessalonians 3:15), yet there later will come a point where they are to be rejected as heathens if they reject the admonition. In his epistle to Titus, Paul draws this distinction: "A man that is an heretick after the first and second admonition reject; Knowing that he that is such is subverted, and sinneth, being condemned of himself" (Titus 3:10–11).

THE PURPOSE OF DISCIPLINE

The true purpose of church discipline is restoration. Paul admonished us in Galatians 6:1 (ESV), "Brothers, if anyone is caught in any transgression, you who are spiritual should restore him in a spirit of gentleness. Keep watch on yourself, lest you too be tempted."

Like all legal processes, church discipline can be abused and misused. But biblical church discipline must always be done in a spirit of edification, not oppression. Indeed, church discipline is to model for us the love of God—God who loves us enough to correct us for our benefit (Hebrews 12).[343] Paul set out the example in 2 Corinthians. In his first epistle to the Corinthians, he had given them instructions to discipline a church member for serious sin and immorality. The discipline was apparently carried out, for in his second epistle to the Corinthians, he speaks of the sinner as repentant and remorseful. Paul's instruction then is to "forgive and comfort him, or he may be overwhelmed by excessive sorrow" (2 Corinthians 2:7 ESV).

A number of purposes are to be accomplished by biblical church discipline. Throughout church history, theologians and pastors numbered their lists differently, but the purposes were consistent. The list offered by the early reformer Martin Bucer in his 1538 book on church discipline is a good example:

> [T]here are five main tasks required in the pastoral office and true care of souls. First: to lead to Christ our Lord and into his communion those who are still estranged from him, whether through carnal excess or false worship. Secondly: to restore those who had once been brought to Christ and into his church but have been drawn away again through the affairs of the flesh or false doctrine. Thirdly: to assist in the true reformation of those who while remaining in the church of Christ have grievously fallen or sinned. Fourthly: to reestablish in true Christian strength those who, while persevering in the fellowship of Christ and not doing anything particularly or grossly wrong, have become somewhat feeble or sick in the Christian life. Fifthly: to protect from all offense and

falling away and continually encourage in all good things those who stay with the flock and in Christ's sheep-pen without grievously sinning or becoming weak and sick in their Christian walk.[344]

We can get a better understanding of these issues by taking a closer look at three purposes for church discipline: protection and purification of the body; impetus for members to take care for their spiritual condition; and blessing upon the one disciplined as that individual is brought to repentance.

First, the body of Christ is protected from being weakened by those who profess Christ but by their acts deny Him. The kingdom of God is vindicated as a holy people when a good testimony of purity is maintained. The Heidelberg Catechism (1563) explained that it was necessary to exclude the "unbelieving and ungodly" from the Lord's supper (see also Matthew 7:6). If they were admitted, "the covenant of God would be profaned, and his wrath kindled against the whole congregation; (a) therefore it is the duty of the Christian church, according to the appointment of Christ and his apostles, to exclude such persons, by the keys of the kingdom of heaven, till they show amendment of life." This teaching is drawn directly from Paul's instructions in 1 Corinthians 11. "Wherefore whosoever shall eat this bread, and drink this cup of the Lord, unworthily, shall be guilty of the body and blood of the Lord" (1 Corinthians 11:27).

The Belgic Confession of 1561 was one of the earliest confessions in the Reformed tradition, and it explained the importance of maintaining a pure church:

> The marks by which the true Church is known are these:
> If the pure doctrine of the gospel is preached therein; if
> she maintains the pure administration of the sacraments
> as instituted by Christ; if church discipline is exercised in

punishing of sin; in short, if all things are managed according to the pure Word of God, all things contrary thereto rejected, and Jesus Christ acknowledged as the only Head of the Church. Hereby the true Church may certainly be known, from which no man has a right to separate himself.[345]

Second, discipline is to spur on those who are spiritually indifferent to repentance and diligence. It is in this way that "evil men are corrected spiritually," as the Belgic Confession put it.[346] "You shall not hate your brother in your heart, but you shall reason frankly with your neighbor, lest you incur sin because of him." (Leviticus 19:17 ESV.)

Third, the offender who is disciplined is benefited if the discipline really does bring him to repentance and restoration. As James wrote, "if any of you do err from the truth, and one convert him; Let him know, that he which converteth the sinner from the error of his way shall save a soul from death, and shall hide a multitude of sins." (James 5:19–20.)

The Helvetic Confession (1566) provided guidance on the purpose of discipline, explaining that discipline was to be done in a spirit of edification rather than oppression. It explained that ministers should "regulate this discipline for edification." It went on to say,

> At all times and in all places the rule is to be observed that everything is to be done for edification, decently and honorably, without oppression and strife. For the apostle testifies that authority in the Church was given to him by the Lord for building up and not for destroying (II Cor. 10:8).

John Calvin also addressed this issue. He explained that church discipline benefited the church, honored Christ, and helped to restore the offenders:

Excommunication is the act by which those who are openly immoral people . . . are rejected from the company of believers, according to God's commandment. In excommunicating them, the church does not mean to cast them into irreparable ruin and despair, but is condemning their life and standards of behavior, and is warning them that they will certainly be damned if they do not change for the better. . . . If wicked people change for the better, the church tenderly receives them afresh both into its fellowship and into the sharing of that unity from which they have been excluded.[347]

CONCLUSION

Hopefully it's clear that church discipline in the Bible is not a heavy-handed tool of punishment. It is instead a process that has all sorts of nuance built in. It applies in ways that fit the situation, from private dispute resolution to public rebuke. Its purposes are to bring a sinner to repentance, to restore that sinner in his or her walk with the Lord and fellowship with the church, and when necessary, to protect the church from danger, discord, and falsehood.

CHAPTER 9 IN A NUTSHELL...

- Jesus has given churches a governmental role through the institution of church discipline.
- The Bible has different procedures for different kinds of discipline.
- The Bible has different levels of discipline.
    - o   Private sins and public sins need different kinds of responses.

- The purposes of discipline are:
  - o Protection
  - o Repentance
  - o Restoration

CHAPTER 10: DISCIPLINE IN CHURCH HISTORY

From the first century on, churches have recognized the necessity of exercising discipline. The methods and manners of discipline have varied, and not everyone agreed on what the appropriate occasions were for exercising discipline. But there has been widespread agreement that the church has the power to police itself.

THE FIRST FEW CENTURIES

We already know from Paul's epistles that church discipline was practiced during the apostolic era. After the close of the New Testament, though, it is hard to get much information. Incidental references to church discipline in the first few centuries of early church history can be pieced together from various documents. Part of the difficulty in analyzing this era arises from the fact that most of the more important documents on discipline were written as apologetic literature. Church discipline only came up as a side issue when the apologists had to defend the church's purity to a pagan readership. As a result, the apologists emphasized the expulsion process and de-emphasized readmission procedures.[348] In any case, we do not always have a full picture.

Historians do know something about controversies that arose in the second and third centuries about when and how to readmit excommunicated people to communion. Church leaders generally agreed that repentance was needed before restoring the person under discipline. But they hotly debated how strict to be in their requirements for demonstrations of repentance and penitence.[349] Indeed, an extremist party opposed any restoration of the sinner. (These extremists were probably adherents of the unorthodox Montanist sect, which claimed direct inspiration from the Holy Spirit.) Moderates advocated various methods of repentance in order to restore a sinner. The standard view in the late second and early third centuries was called *exomologesis*. It allowed restoration to communion if the sinner had both "consciousness" of guilt and some accompanying penitential act indicating their repentance.[350] These controversies indicate plainly enough that excommunication was a widely used sanction—what to do after it was the question.

By the fourth century, we get a clearer picture. It seems that the most common solution was to readmit members after they carried out some public act of penance. The bishop would determine the length of time for penance, and would make the official decision to readmit a penitent. But as time went on, the rigors of public penance grew increasingly onerous. Bishops could mandate celibacy, or sexual abstinence even if already married; prohibit holding public office or serving in the military; even limit attendance at public functions like games and feasts. And these could be lifelong requirements. These were heavy penalties indeed, going far beyond anything implied in Scripture. The church eventually began to loosen up, and around the sixth century, the practice of "private penance" via confession was introduced.[351]

ROMAN CATHOLIC CHURCH IN THE MEDIEVAL ERA

As the church entered the Middle Ages, private confession to a clergyman became the primary means of maintaining church purity and exercising church discipline. According to the medieval scholastic theologians, the clergy could hear the penitent and pronounce the forgiveness of sins. If there was some major sin issue, it might go to an ecclesiastical court. Excommunication was a last resort, only imposed if the offender did not obey the court orders.[352]

In the thirteenth century, a church council established the rule that confession had to happen at least annually. In an era when much of the church's work was done in Latin and not understood by the common people, this requirement of meeting with the priest at least once a year was significant. It was one of the few ways of actually making sure that the church's morality and doctrine were understood and applied by laymen.[353]

Details of the Roman Catholic Church's theology and practice of discipline evolved over time, but the sacrament of penance became a solid part of that church's doctrine. To this day, the Roman Catholic Church holds church disciplinary power in high regard. It recognizes that "the disciplinary power of the Church is a . . . practical application, of its power of jurisdiction, and includes the various forms of . . . legislative, administrative, judicial, and coercive power."[354]

THE REFORMATION OF CHURCH DISCIPLINE

Church discipline, penitence, and all the other issues and practices surrounding it were important parts of medieval society.[355] The Reformation had to work through these issues and address them. It was not an easy process. The Reformation's leading minds had to reexamine and untangle centuries of accumulated tradition, theology, and teaching as they tried to settle on an approach to church discipline based on *sola scriptura*—the authority of Scripture alone.

The Protestants came to basic agreements that confession to a clergyman was not necessary to obtain right standing with God and that clergy should proclaim the gospel of salvation through Christ rather than presume to proclaim forgiveness of sins. But there were all sorts of debates and discussions. What was the place of private confession? What about public confession? How should the clergy deal with people who still wanted to come and confess sins? What was the standard for excommunication? Who should have the final say?

The Protestants had a different view of Matthew 16, with its text on the "keys of the kingdom," than the Catholic view. During the Medieval period, Roman Catholic theologians came to interpret the power of the keys in Matthew 16 as a specific grant of authority to Peter that was then preserved in the office of the pope.[356] The power of the priest to proclaim the absolution of sins after confession was considered the exercise of the "power of the keys." Protestants, by contrast, understood Matthew 16 as a grant of power to the church in general, not to a specific church hierarchy or individual (certainly not the papacy).[357]

There was some argument among the Reformers about what "binding and loosing" meant. Martin Luther believed that it referred to "public" binding and loosing (as per Matthew 18) through the excommunication of unrepentant sinners.[358] The Swiss Reformer Zwingli interpreted the passage as calling for the church's proclamation of the gospel that has the power to bind and loose individuals from sins.[359] But however this passage was interpreted, the Reformers always recognized that there was a duty on the church to maintain its purity through discipline.

Amidst all the uncertainty and soul-searching, the Reformation did not reject the power of the church to exercise discipline. To the contrary, it reaffirmed it. John Calvin spoke for many of the Reformers when he wrote, "As the saving measure of Christ is the soul of the church, so its discipline is like the sinews by which the members of the body each in its place are held together."[360] The Reformers recognized that there had to be methods of accountability, and even sanctions on misconduct, so that the church would be "held together" in purity.

THE PROTESTANT POSITION ON CHURCH DISCIPLINE

In his epistle to the Corinthians, Paul admonished the church that discipline within the church was its duty: "For what have I to do to judge them also that are without? do not ye judge them that are within? But them that are without God judgeth. Therefore put away from among yourselves that wicked person." (1 Corinthians 5:12–13) Paul sharply rebuked the church for not taking care of its internal matters (1 Corinthians 6:1–6). "Dare any of you, having a matter against another, go to law before the unjust, and not before the saints? Do ye not know that the saints shall judge the world? and if the world shall be judged by you, are ye unworthy to judge the smallest matters?" (1 Corinthians 6: 1–2). He asked rhetorically, "Is it so, that there is not a wise man among you? no, not one that shall be able to judge between his brethren?" (1 Corinthians 6:5).

The Protestant churches took Paul's teaching seriously. They recognized that church discipline was an important task and duty of a well-functioning church. The historic Protestant views on church discipline can be ascertained from the many confessions, catechisms, and other doctrinal statements that were drafted, especially in the Reformation era.

THE POWER OF THE KEYS

Many of the Protestant confessions mentioned the "power of the keys" as a crucial part of the church's responsibility. (We have already referred to a number of these confessions in our discussion of the restorative purpose of discipline in chapter 9.) The most important confession of the Lutheran Reformation, the Augsburg Confession of 1530, explained the Protestant view of the power of the keys: "But this is their opinion, that the power of the Keys, or the power of the bishops, according to the Gospel, is a power or commandment of God, to preach the Gospel, to remit and retain sins, and to administer Sacraments."

The Second Helvetic Confession of 1566 was one of the most widely influential early Reformed confessions. It viewed discipline as "an absolute necessity" and cited the long history of discipline in the church:

> And since discipline is an absolute necessity in the
> Church and excommunication was once used in the time
> of the early fathers, and there were ecclesiastical judg-
> ments among the people of God, wherein this discipline
> was exercised by wise and godly men, it also falls to
> ministers to regulate this discipline for edification, ac-
> cording to the circumstances of the time, public state, and
> necessity.

Similarly, the Church of England's Thirty-Nine Articles of Religion (1563) recognized the power and responsibility of the church to maintain purity and discipline. The articles, which established the basic tenets of the Anglican confession, note that this duty includes ensuring good discipline among the clergy as well as everyone else: "Nevertheless, it appertaineth to the discipline of the Church, that inquiry be made of evil Ministers, and that they be accused by those that have knowledge of their offences; and finally, being found guilty, by just judgment be deposed."[361]

The great Westminster Confession of 1647 (still the confession of many Presbyterians around the world) addressed church discipline in detail. It began the section, interestingly enough, by acknowledging that Jesus, "as king and head of His Church," has ordained that the church have a government "distinct from the civil magistrate."[362] God committed to the church government the "keys of the kingdom," the Confession said. It went on to explain the kinds of disciplinary practices and the purposes for which they were to be used.[363]

Finally, the London Baptist Confession (1689) echoed the Westminster Confession on a great many points (though differing on details of the form of church government and on the issues of baptism).

It stated, "As all believers are bound to join themselves to particular churches, when and where they have opportunity so to do; so all that are admitted unto the privileges of a church, are also under the censures and government thereof, according to the rule of Christ."[364]

John Calvin stated the matter most succinctly: "It is the Word of God which gives authority to condemn the perverse, just as it gives authority to receive into favour those who mend their ways."[365]

THE STEPS OF MATTHEW 18

Many of the Protestant statements on church discipline were drawn straight from the instructions of Christ in Matthew 18. They outlined the discipline process to be followed in the Reformed churches, referring to the three steps that the Messiah gave.

The Heidelberg Catechism of 1563 was one of the most widely used instructional tools of the Reformed churches. It is still the creed of a number of Reformed denominations around the world. Question 85 in the catechism asks, "How is the kingdom of heaven shut and opened by Christian discipline?" The answer is that it is to be done "according to the command of Christ," and the command given in Matthew 18 is then described. When wrong doctrines or practices arise among those who claim the "name of Christians," they should be, first, "brotherly admonished." If they do not then "renounce their errors and wicked course of life," they can be "complained of to the church, or to those, who are thereunto appointed by the church." "[I]f they despise their admonition," they may then be "forbidden the use of the sacraments; whereby they are excluded from the Christian church, and by God himself from the kingdom of Christ; and when they promise and show real amendment, are again received as members of Christ and his church."[366]

This emphasis on "brotherly admonition," on repentance, and on restoration was echoed repeatedly in the Reformation's writings on discipline: in the *Book of Discipline* that John Knox helped to draft, in the Church of England's Thirty-Nine Articles of Religion (1563), in the Savoy Declaration of 1658, and in the Irish Articles of Religion (1615), to mention a few.

Going forward more than a century and a half, we find the principles repeated yet again. An 1817 publication of the African Methodist Episcopal Church addressed church disciplinary functions, again closely tracking Christ's outline in Matthew 18. Particularly interesting is a list of the types of subjects that were considered appropriate for discipline—they were not limited to what many today would think of as "moral" offenses. Extensive provisions were made for adjudicating issues arising from church members accused of defaulting on debts and in disputes over other business matters.[367]

THE DECLINE OF DISCIPLINE

The overwhelming weight of serious Christian ecclesiology has recognized the importance of church discipline throughout church history. Grounded in Scripture and practiced in history, perhaps the most remarkable thing about the practice of church discipline is that it is not better understood in the modern church. Albert Mohler, Jr., president of Southern Baptist Theological Seminary, wrote in 1998, "The decline of church discipline is perhaps the most visible failure of the contemporary church."[368]

In the course of time, there would always be periods in which some people backed off from taking the firm line on church discipline. While we are certainly living in such a time today, this is not the first time. In 1852, James Boyce, the founder of the Southern Baptist Theological Seminary, wrote that many American churches were relaxing or even discounting church discipline, ignoring the biblical and historic position of the church:

It has been customary, among certain classes of
Christians, to deny to the church the possession of this
power. But such assertions are made in utter disregard of
the language in which Christ authorized His disciples
to bind and to loose . . . as well as in disregard of the recorded action of the apostolic churches.[369]

Boyce feared for the future integrity of the church. He concluded:
"Could it be exercised throughout our church with the constancy and
strictness that marked them in days gone by, we might look with assur-
ance for similar spirituality in the church; and for additional efficiency in
its present and future efforts for Christ."[370]

But a century later, American churches in many denominations still
were uninterested in church discipline. Or, in some cases, they were
afraid of it. In 1985, a commission on theology and church relations
of the Lutheran Church, Missouri Synod, issued an important study of
the status of discipline in the Lutheran tradition.[371] The commission
concluded that the exercise of church discipline was a biblical duty of
the church. It noted that Martin Luther, Phillip Melancthon, and the
early Lutheran confessions recognized church discipline as an important
requirement for a well-ordered church. The commission reported a
decline in the exercise of discipline in its own denomination and offered
an important corrective to those who feared that the exercise of discipline
would turn people off:

> [One] reason for the decline of church discipline is to
> be found in a fear of criticism or in the fear of the loss
> of members. "What will people think of us" if we really
> begin to get serious also in this aspect of our life together?
> How can we attract people to the Gospel of the Lord
> Jesus Christ when we appear loveless in our attitude even
> toward those who are members of the church? Won't

people go elsewhere if their doctrine or morals are questioned by the church? Isn't it better for the sake of our ministry to them to forget about church discipline? At least then we will have some chance of gaining them for Christ.

But the commission realized that these fears were misguided:

A few minutes' reflection should reveal the fallacy of such points of view. We dare never base our course of action on what others may think rather than on a genuine concern both for the will of the Lord and for those whose souls are . . . in jeopardy.[372]

As a matter of biblical theology and pastoral counsel, the commission was absolutely right. But one issue remains that the commission did not address: the legal issue. This wasn't a great concern in the mid-1980s, but it is today. But thanks to the church autonomy doctrine, American churches have robust legal protections when they handle disciplinary matters properly.

CHAPTER 10 IN A NUTSHELL...

- Throughout church history, Christians have recognized that church discipline is an important responsibility.
- The Protestant Reformers wrote a lot about the importance of biblical church discipline and how it should be done.
- The practice of church discipline has declined in recent years
  - o in part because we don't know the biblical importance of discipline, and
  - o in part because we're afraid of getting in trouble for practicing church discipline.

CHAPTER 11: PRACTICAL STEPS FOR PROTECTION

The current law on church autonomy provides substantial protection to churches practicing church discipline—as long as the churches fulfill their responsibilities. By thoughtfully applying biblical principles of church government and church discipline, churches reduce their legal risks. In this chapter, we'll explain most important steps that churches can take to protect themselves.[373]

CHURCH GOVERNMENT: DON'T MAKE IT UP AS YOU GO

First, on all sorts of intrachurch conflicts and disputes, a church is much more likely to get the protection of the church autonomy doctrine if the church government structure was in place at the time that the discipline procedure was initiated. It is important that the proper procedures were followed, with the appropriate church leadership making the decisions.

This, in turn, means that it is important for churches to really know who makes what decisions in the congregation. It would be wise for any church to have written documents that explain the church government and procedures. They should spell this out clearly and understandably to their members in some sort of church covenant or constitution. In some situations, what passes for a "church" is merely a meeting of people with one or more de facto leaders who might preach or counsel the others. But such casual associations do not even meet the definition of a church articulated by the Reformers. They listed three basic marks of a true church: first, the word of God is preached. Second, the sacraments are administered faithfully. Third, the church is subject to biblical church discipline. If we are going to embrace these biblical marks of a church, we should be able to say so clearly in a church's constituting documents. Failing to do so creates confusion among the members, and chaos in the courts.

The common sense step of explaining what a church is and how it is run can make an important difference if a church is called to account before a state or federal court. In many cases, the courts have viewed it as significant that church members knew the church's position on discipline and church government when they joined the church.[374] For instance, if church members do not have some clear idea of who makes what decisions, then a court will have a much more difficult job from the outset, as it tries to determine whether the church is operating as a church, as opposed to, say, a social club.

CLEAR MEMBERSHIP REQUIREMENTS

Second, a church should have clearly defined membership requirements. A clear position on church membership makes clear what is happening in a church discipline action, because both congregants and leaders know who is really accountable. Moreover, if a church does not have membership requirements, and it tries to excommunicate someone, the question arises: What are they being excommunicated from? If they are simply being told to leave a casual get-together or a social club, no church autonomy issues are involved. Of course, the Bible teaches that the church is never merely a social club. And if the issue ends up in court, the courts have viewed it as significant that people voluntarily entered into membership in a church. The courts are then much more likely to find that church autonomy protections apply to the church.[375]

CLEAR DOCTRINAL BASIS FOR ACTION

Third, particularly on the issue of church discipline, the church should be sure to have a clear theological basis for any action that it decides to take. Church autonomy legal protection only comes into play when the issue really does involve a church's ability to apply doctrine.[376] On this point, it would be advisable to make the biblical basis of church discipline procedures clear in the written documents.

It would also be wise for congregations to have some synopsis of the standards of conduct expected of members. This avoids the possibility that the church member might later plead ignorance.[377] In order to avoid confusion later on, church leaders should be careful about promising absolute confidentiality to anyone. In Matthew 18, the standard operating procedure for dealing with private sins is to begin with one-on-one confrontation and discussion, which would of course be confidential. But if this private attempt at reconciliation does not bear fruit, there may be the need to involve other church elders, and if this is not successful, it will ultimately be necessary to involve the entire church. If a pastor promises absolute confidentiality early on in the process, he might find it very awkward to get the additional people involved who need to be involved.[378]

DOCUMENTATION

Fourth, there should be adequate documentation of the discipline process. This needs to be done with care. On the one hand, it is not helpful to start putting things in writing too soon. Writings stay around and are permanent; hurtful things said in writing are remembered. On the other hand, if and when the time comes for a formal, final step in the discipline process—namely, excommunication—it needs to be done with an appropriately formal statement, and one should be made in writing.

A mere phone call leaves no record. In court, it becomes a matter of "he said/she said." Churches should be prepared for the fact that the excommunicated person who is disgruntled enough to go to court very likely would also attempt to bring a case to the public via blogs and social networking sites. Any documentation—such as a letter of excommunication—could easily end up posted online. Church leaders writing the letter should be aware of this and craft a letter that explains the matter well enough so that it can in fact serve as a protection for the church—demonstrating that the church followed proper procedure for some legitimate cause.

COMMON SENSE...AND BIBLICAL SENSE

Finally, the non-legal aspects should never be overlooked. The purpose of church discipline is to restore, not to penalize. Make every effort to see repentance happen at the early stages of confrontation, before there has to be a public proceeding. And in the process, church leaders should be willing to admit a genuine mistake, but not to compromise biblical convictions.

We have already seen that there is a substantial biblical and historical basis for the practice of church discipline. As churches face new challenges to this ability, the church autonomy doctrine becomes increasingly important. Professor Richard Garnett has said it well: "the preservation of the churches' moral and legal right to govern themselves in accord with their own norms and in response to their own calling is our day's most pressing religious freedom challenge."[379]

Thankfully, most courts still do respect and protect the legitimate exercise of this responsibility by the church. The words of an old court decision continue to ring true today:

> We have no right, and, therefore, will not exercise the

power, to dictate ecclesiastical law. We do not aspire to become de facto heads of the church, and, by construction or otherwise, abrogate its laws and canons. We shall not inquire whether the alleged omission is any offense. This is a question of ecclesiastical cognizance. This is no forum for such adjudication. The church should guard its own fold; enact and construe its own laws; enforce its own discipline; and thus will be maintained the boundary between the temporal and spiritual power.[380]

CHAPTER 11 IN A NUTSHELL...

- Churches will usually get legal protection:
  - o When they have set up a clear structure for the church government
  - o When they have clear membership standards
  - o When they have a clear doctrinal basis for any action they take
  - o When they appropriately document proceedings

CHAPTER 12: CONCLUSION

Our journey is now complete. We began by looking at the revival of churches that dare to exercise church discipline. This phenomenon is often misunderstood by outside observers—such as the news reporters who wonder at the renewal of the "ancient" practice, and the disgruntled congregants who prefer to sue their pastors rather than face the church. But we also recognized that more was involved when churches get sued than just a messy church argument. To get the perspective we need, we have taken a historical look at church discipline, that governmental function of the church maintaining its purity. We learned that this practice has been important to the integrity of the church for generations. We have seen that church discipline is not meant to be harsh or vengeful, but is rather practiced out of love and concern for the body of Christ.

We have looked anew at the relationship between church government and civil government, getting a fresh perspective on the separation of church and state. In the process we saw that it was the exercise of church discipline itself that forced the refinement of church-state relations at crucial times in history. The separation of church and state, at its heart, is all about the proper biblical relationships between these two God-ordained, but independent, institutions.

Finally, we returned to the contemporary issues surrounding church discipline, this time approaching the questions from the legal perspective as we described the important doctrine of church autonomy. Church autonomy provides important legal protections for churches today. In doing so, it reflects centuries of theological reflection on the relationship between church and state, and it does so surprisingly well in many cases.

What can we take away from this journey? First, church discipline, when properly practiced, is a time-honored necessary protection for the integrity of the church. Second, the practice of church discipline forces us to recognize that the word "government" applies to more than just the civil government. God has created a plurality of jurisdictions in the world, for our protection and blessing. The church and the state exist side by side as government institutions. Third, we see that throughout history, there has been a struggle for a biblical balance between these two institutions. We have argued that the Reformation offered key insights for a proper relationship, and that those insights eventually made their way into the First Amendment of the U.S. Constitution.

We have learned that the notion of two kingdoms, church and state, as equals operating in distinct jurisdictions, is a theological concept with roots extending back almost three thousand years to the Old Testament. This doctrine was recognized in the church of antiquity and then received its most significant development (from an American perspective especially) in the Protestant Reformation. Reformation thought, and particularly Calvinistic thought, recognized church and state as institutionally separate entities—both under God, but neither usurping the administration of the other. We have seen that these principles are now embodied in the legal doctrine of church autonomy. The legal doctrine of church autonomy has had its ups and downs and has not always been applied consistently. But the overall tenor of the decisions, and the philosophy that the autonomy doctrine embodies, remains strikingly consistent with the "two kingdoms" theology from which it grew. And the doctrine retains as much vitality as ever in the courts.[381]

The issue has always been jurisdictional. Is the state all-powerful? Or are there limits to the state's reach? If there are limits, then it follows that there are jurisdictions other than the state. As one scholar has written, "If churches are not independent of the state, if they are not free to be different from the state, and if the government is not limited by churches' freedom, then believers are not really free, either."[382] Another scholar explained, "Without church autonomy, civil society will lose organized religion as a check and limit on the pretensions of Caesar. And that would surely lead to a more authoritarian state. Whether one is personally religious or not, we all have a liberty stake in that not happening."[383]

That there is a multiplicity of jurisdictions follows from the biblical belief, proclaimed so boldly by the Reformation, that only God is sovereign and all-powerful, and thus no human institution can be either all-powerful or "sovereign" in an absolute sense. Personal liberty follows from this limit on human institutions. For these reasons, an understanding of church autonomy cases comes near to the very root of freedom. By understanding this, we can better appreciate the goals of church autonomy and its message of "spheres of sovereignty."[384]

APPENDIX: RESOURCES FOR FURTHER STUDY

1. FURTHER READING ON CHURCH DISCIPLINE AND CHURCH GOVERNMENT

Adams, Jay E. *Handbook of Church Discipline*. Grand Rapids: Zondervan, 1986.

Bucer, Martin. *Concerning the True Care of Souls.* Trans. Peter Beale. Edinburgh: Banner of Truth, 2009.

Dever, Mark. *Nine Marks of a Healthy Church*. Wheaton, Illinois: Crossway Books, 2000.

House, H. Wayne. *Christian Ministries and the Law.* Rev. ed. Grand Rapids: Kregel, 1999.

House, H. Wayne. "Church Discipline and the Courts." *Southern Baptist Journal of Theology* 4 (2000): 60–75. Available on-line at http://www.sbts.edu/resources/journal-of-theology/sbjt-44-winter-2000/church-discipline-and-the-courts/.

Juster, Daniel. *Due Process.* Shippensburg, Pennsylvania: Destiny Image, 1992.

Leeman, Jonathan. *The Church and the Surprising Offense of God's Love: Reintroducing the Doctrines of Church Membership and Discipline.* Wheaton: Crossway, 2010.

Leeman, Jonathan. *Church Discipline: How the Church Protects the Name of Jesus.* Wheaton: Crossway, 2012.

2. PRACTICAL LEGAL GUIDANCE FOR CHURCHES

The Alliance Defending Freedom, a legal advocacy organization specializing in religious freedom issues, provides a wealth of practical resources for churches at their website: *speakupmovement.org/Church.* Their resources are especially helpful for churches that want to draft bylaws and other governing documents that will provide legal protection. As we go to press, the direct link to church resources is: *http://speakupmovement. org/Church/LearnMore/Details/3767.*

3. FURTHER READING ON THE HISTORY OF CHURCH AND STATE

Benedict, Philip. *Christ's Churches Purely Reformed: A Social History of Calvinism.* New Haven and London: Yale University Press, 2002

Berman, Harold. *Law and Revolution.* Cambridge: Harvard University Press, 1983.

Dreisbach, Daniel L. *Thomas Jefferson and the Wall of Separation between Church and State.* New York: New York University Press, 2002.

Eidsmoe, John. *God and Caesar.* Westchester, Illinois: Crossway Books, 1984.

George Gillespie, *Aaron's Rod Blossoming* (reprint, Harrisonburg, Virginia: Sprinkle, 1985) (1646).

Hall, David W. *The Genevan Reformation and the American Founding.* Lanham, Maryland: Lexington, 2003.

Hutson, James H. *Religion and the Founding of the American Republic.* Washington, D.C.: Library of Congress, 1998.

Kelly, Douglas. *The Emergence of Liberty in the Modern World: The Influence of Calvin on Five Governments from the 16th Through 18th Centuries.* Philipsburg, New Jersey: Presbyterian and Reformed, 1992.

Witte, John, Jr. *Law and Protestantism.* Cambridge: Cambridge University Press, 2002.

Witte, John, Jr. *The Reformation of Rights.* Cambridge: Cambridge University Press, 2007.

ACKNOWLEDGMENTS

It has been four years since we first started writing this book. As we write this, it is sometimes hard to believe that we are nearly done. Actually, "done" might be the wrong word. We are continually discovering new material; the book would keep growing if it weren't for the fact that, at some point, we have to stop.

Looking back on the journey we've travelled, it is a pleasure to acknowledge the family, friends, and mentors who made this book possible and encouraged us along the way. Our friend Doug Phillips got us started writing on the subject of church autonomy. His love for the freedom and purity of Christ's church has been an inspiration. The editors of the Northern Kentucky Law Review gave us a place to publish our first research. Three distinguished scholars, Nicholas Wolterstorff, John Mansfield, and John Witte, encouraged us greatly by telling us that we were onto something with the subject of church autonomy. It meant a great deal to hear this from scholars of their caliber. Pastor William Einwechter played a key role in encouraging us to turn our law review article into something for church leaders.

Once we started writing the book, many friends generously gave of their time to read, review, and help us refine our manuscript: Robert Barth, John Eidsmoe, David Hall, Daniel Juster, Jeffrey Tuomala, Bret Kendall, Steve Leston, and John Mauck. Mark Weaver gave us early editorial advice. Wesley Strackbein provided a sounding board for ideas throughout the writing process. Tom Ertl and Jean-Marc Berthoud introduced us to the contributions of the reformer Pierre Viret. Allen Smith—attorney, church elder, and friend—hospitably gave us the use of his law offices for several days of writing. David Hall, Steve Leston, and Doug Wilson provided us with valuable advice about publishing. Our friends Isaac Botkin and Chris Leclerc have been incredibly generous with their time and talents in helping us with design and production. Mark Sutherland of Dunrobin Publishing believed in our book project enough to publish it; he has been a pleasure to work with.

Our families have been our most steady source of support and encouragement. Lael's wife, Sarah, has advised on every aspect of the book. His parents, David and Betty Weinberger, have been wonderful editors, as has his mother-in-law, Teresa Cook. Bob's parents have been great cheer leaders and provided prayer support through the entire process. It is to our parents that we gratefully dedicate this book.

If we were to try to name everyone who has blessed us along the way, this book would become much too long. To all of these friends and family, named and unnamed, we say a heartfelt "thank you." We hope and pray that this book is a blessing to others. Soli Deo gloria.

ABOUT THE AUTHORS

Robert J. Renaud graduated from Oak Brook College of Law with his law degree in 2009. A former speechwriter and researcher, he is now the third generation to work with his family's manufacturing company in St. Louis, Missouri.

Lael D. Weinberger also received a law degree from Oak Brook College of Law. After graduating, he clerked for the Idaho Supreme Court. He is now practicing law and pursuing graduate studies in history.

INDEX

NOTES

INTRODUCTION

1. The facts that follow are taken from the court decision, Westbrook v. Penley, 231 S.W.3d 389 (Tex. 2007).

2. Robert Joseph Renaud and Lael Daniel Weinberger, "Spheres of Sovereignty: Church Autonomy Doctrine and the Theological Heritage of the Separation of Church and State," *Northern Kentucky Law Review* 35 (2008): 67–102.

3. "Woman Says Church Threatening To Make Sins Public," News4Jax, Jacksonville, Florida, 15 December 2008, http://www.news4jax.com/news/18286355/detail.html (last visited 11 February 2009).

4. The story was carried on the local television station, *id.*, and on Fox News: Diane Macedo, "Florida Woman Says Former Church Plans to Make Her Sins Public," Fox News, 18 December 2008, http://www.foxnews.com/story/0,2933,469928,00.html (last visited 11 February 2009).

5. Alexandra Alter, "Banned from Church," *Wall Street Journal*, January 18, 2008, online at http://online.wsj.com/article/SB120061470848399079.

6. See also Scott C. Idleman, "Tort Liability, Religious Entities, and the Decline of Constitutional Protection," *Indiana Law Journal* 75 (2000): 219, 240–44; H. Wayne House, *Christian Ministries and the Law* (rev. ed., Grand Rapids: Kregel, 1999), 65–66.

7. Mark A. Weitz, *Clergy Malpractice in America* (Lawrence: University Press of Kansas, 2001).

8. The case is *Nally v. Grace Community Church*, 763 P.2d 948 (Cal. 1988). Church autonomy did not decide the case (it was hardly even mentioned), so the California court's decision did not set a particularly helpful precedent for church discipline cases in general. The court did allude to church autonomy considerations in dicta: "Because of the differing theological views espoused by

the myriad of religions in our state and practiced by church members, it would certainly be impractical, and quite possibly unconstitutional, to impose a duty of care on pastoral counselors. Such a duty would necessarily be intertwined with the religious philosophy of the particular denomination or ecclesiastical teachings of the religious entity."

CHAPTER 1

9. R.L. Dabney, *The Practical Philosophy* (1897; photo. reprint 1984), 394.

10. Newdow lost his case in the U.S. Supreme Court on standing issues. Elk Grove Unified School District v. Newdow, 542 U.S. 1 (2003).

11. See, e.g., Carol Cratty, "Lawsuit seeks to take 'so help me God' out of inaugural," CNN News, 31 December 2008, http://www.cnn.com/2008/POLITICS/12/31/inauguration.lawsuit/ (last visited 21 June 2012).

12. Steven B. Epstein, "Rethinking the Constitutionality of Ceremonial Deism," *Columbia Law Review* 96 (1996): 2083, 2106–2111.

13. Newdow v. Roberts, 603 F. 3d 1002 (D.C. Circ. 2010).

14. Richard Browser and Robin Muse, "Historical Perspectives on Church and State," in Ann W. Duncan and Steven L. Jones, eds. *Church-State Issues in America Today* (Westport, Connecticut: Greenwood Publishing Group 2008), 48. See also Paul Horwitz, *The Agnostic Age: Law, Religion, and the Constitution* (New York: Oxford University Press, 2011), 22–38.

15. Our focus in this book is on reclaiming the forgotten, positive heritage of the "separation of church and state," so we won't spend much time on the kinds of issues that so often capture headlines, like public Ten Commandments displays or prayer at inaugurations. But we certainly agree that the "strict separationist" position is problematic. More broadly, efforts to exclude religion from public life are a dangerous form of intolerance. On the subject of religion in public life generally, see Stephen L. Carter, *The Culture of Disbelief* (New York: Basic Books, 1993).

16. See John Witte, Jr., "The Essential Rights and Liberties of Religion in the American Constitutional Experiment," *Notre Dame Law Review* 71 (1996): 372; John Witte, Jr., *The Reformation of Rights* (Cambridge: Cambridge University Press, 2007), 277–319; David S. Clark, "The Medieval Origins of Modern Legal Education: Between Church and State," *American Journal of Comparative Law* 35 (1987): 653 (1987); John Witte, Jr., "That Serpentine Wall of Separation," *Michigan Law Review* 101 (2003): 1869–1905.

17.   See Daniel L. Dreisbach, *Thomas Jefferson and the Wall of Separation between Church and State* (New York: New York University Press, 2002).

18.   *See* Herbert W. Titus, *God, Man, and Law* (Oak Brook: IBLP, 1994), 65.

19.   *See also Mark* 12: 13–17; *Luke* 20:21–25 (parallel accounts). And for additional commentary on the implications of Christ's statement for legal and political theory, see Titus, *God, Man, and Law*, 65.

20.   Matthew 22:21 (ESV).

21.   John Calvin, *Commentary on a Harmony of the Evangelists*, William Pringle, trans. (1846; photo. reprint 2005) 3:45.

22.   Matthew 22:21 (ESV).

23.   See also Michael W. McConnell, "Religion and Constitutional Rights: Why is Religious Liberty the 'First Freedom'?," *Cardozo Law Review* 21 (2000): 1243, 1246 (the notion of two kingdoms is the "most powerful possible refutation of the notion that the political sphere is omnicompetent").

24.   Calvin, *Commentary on a Harmony of the Evangelists*, 45.

25.   John Gill, *Exposition of the New Testament* (1809), 1:258. For biographical background on Gill, see generally John Rippon, *Life and Writings of the Rev. John Gill* (1838).

26.   John Calvin, *Commentaries on the Epistles of Paul the Apostle to the Philippians, Colossians, and Thessalonians*, John Pringle, trans. (1851; photo. reprint 2005), 152.

27.   *See* John Calvin, *Institutes of the Christian Religion*, Henry Beveridge, trans. (Grand Rapids: Eerdmans, 1979), 4.11. *See also* Westminster Confession of Faith XXIII, III (1646); Westminster Shorter Catechism XXXI, II (1647); Heidelberg Catechism 83 (1563); Augsburg Confession, Art. XXVIII (1530), in *Triglot Concordia: The Symbolical Books of the Evangelical Lutheran Church*, F. Bente and W. H. T. Dau, trans. (St. Louis: Concordia, 1921).

28.   See Witte, "That Serpentine Wall of Separation," 1876; Greg L. Bahnsen, *Theonomy in Christian Ethics* (3d ed., Nacogdoches, Texas: Covenant Media Press, 2002), 389–419.

29.   The office of judge was established in Exodus 18:13–26, while the office of priest was created in Exodus 28:1.

30.   See Bahnsen, 389.

31.   1 Samuel 13:9–14.

32.   2 Chronicles 26:16.

33. See, e.g., Exodus 30:7–8, Numbers 4:16.

34. 2 Chronicles 26:18 (ESV).

35. *See 2 Chronicles* 18:3–6.

36. John Gill, *Exposition of the Old Testament* (London: Mathews and Leigh, 1810), 3:67.

37. *Oxford English Dictionary* (2nd ed. 1989), s.v., "jurisdiction"; *Webster's New World Dictionary* (2nd ed., 1986), s.v., "jurisdiction," "diction".

38. Romans 13:4.

39. Johan D. van der Vyver, "The Jurisprudential Legacy of Abraham Kuyper and Leo XII," *Journal of Markets & Morality* 5 (2002):211, 212–13. For readings from Groen van Prinsterer on sphere sovereignty, see Guillaume Groen van Prinsterer, "Unbelief and Revolution" (1847), in James W. Skillen and Rockne W. McCarthy, eds., *Political Order and the Plural Structure of Society* (Atlanta: Scholars Press, 1991), 65.

40. For more on Abraham Kuyper and sphere sovereignty, see Peter S. Heslam, *Creating a Christian Worldview: Abraham Kuyper's Lectures on Calvinism* (Grand Rapids: Eerdmans, 1998); James D. Bratt, "Introduction," *in* James D. Bratt, ed., *Abraham Kuyper: A Centennial Reader* (Grand Rapids: Eerdmans, 1998); Abraham Kuyper, "Sphere Sovereignty" (October 20, 1880), *in* Bratt, ed., *Centennial Reader*; Abraham Kuyper, *Lectures on Calvinism* (Grand Rapids: Eerdmans, 1943); van der Vyver, "The Jurisprudential Legacy of Abraham Kuyper and Leo XII," *Journal of Markets & Morality* 5 (2002):211, 212–13; Paul Horwitz, Churches as First Amendment Institutions: Of Sovereignty and Spheres, *Harvard Civil Rights-Civil Liberties Law Review* 44 (2009): 79. A draft version of Horwitz's article is available online at SSRN: http://ssrn.com/abstract=1285328. See also Lael Daniel Weinberger, "The Business Judgment Rule and Sphere Sovereignty," *Thomas Cooley Law Review* 27 (2010): 279–319 (discussing the theory of sphere sovereignty and applying its concepts to a business law issue).

41. David K. Naugle, *Worldview: The History of a Concept* (Grand Rapids: Eerdmans, 2002), 37–39, 46–50; Bratt, "Introduction," to Bratt, ed., *Abraham Kuyper: A Centennial Reader*, 13.

42. The lectures are printed as Abraham Kuyper, *Lectures on Calvinism* (Grand Rapids: Eerdmans, 1943).

43. For a more detailed exposition of Kuyper's thought on this topic, see the excellent article by Nicholas Wolterstorff, "Abraham Kuyper on the Limited Authority of Church and State," *Georgetown Journal of Law and Public Policy* 7

(2009): 105.

44.   Kuyper, *Lectures*, 79 (emphasis in original).

45.   Kuyper, *Lectures*, 90, 96, 98; see also Herman Dooyeweerd, "The Christian Idea of the State," in *Essays in Legal, Social, and Political Philosophy*, John Kraay trans. (Lewiston, New York: Edwin Mellen Press 1996), 155; R.J. Rushdoony, *This Independent Republic* (Nutley, New Jersey: Craig Press, 1964), 33–40, 146–51.

46.   Kuyper, *Lectures*, 164.

47.   Kuyper, *Lectures*, 116. It is worth noting that part of Kuyper's unique perspective was extending this analysis of social spheres beyond just the church, the state, and even the family, which are the basic biblically-recognized governmental structures. He also applied this theological analysis to business, art, academia, and all other social institutional fields. For further discussion of Kuyper's ideas and how they relate to church-state issues in particular, see Wolterstorff, "Abraham Kuyper on the Limited Authority of Church and State."

48.   Kuyper, *Lectures*, 166.

49.   McConnell, "Religion and Constitutional Rights: Why is Religious Liberty the 'First Freedom'?," 1246.

50.   Carter, *Culture of Disbelief*, 134.

CHAPTER 2

51.   See James J. O'Donnell, *Augustine: A New Biography* (New York: HarperCollins, 2005), 9–12. As Augustine's translator wrote, "After more than eleven hundred years of steady and triumphant progress, Rome had been taken and sacked. It is difficult for us to appreciate . . . the shock which was thus communicated from centre to circumference of the whole known world." Marcus Dods, "Translator's Preface," to Saint Augustine, *A Select Library of the Nicene and Post-Nicene Fathers of the Christian Church*, Vol. II, *St. Augustin's City of God and Christian Doctrine*, ed. Philip Schaff, (Buffalo: Christian Literature Co., 1887).

52.   John Witte, Jr., "That Serpentine Wall of Separation," *Michigan Law Review* 101 (2003):1878.

53.   Witte, "That Serpentine Wall of Separation," 1878.

54.   Augustine died in 430; Gelasius was pope from 492 to 496.

55.   Norman F. Cantor, *The Civilization of the Middle Ages*, rev. ed. (New York:

HarperCollins, 1993), 86–87.

56. Harold J. Berman, *Law and Revolution* (Cambridge: Harvard University Press, 1983), 92. See also Arthur Hyman, *Philosophy in the Middle Ages* (Indianapolis : Hackett, 1983), 715. The full text of the letter, as printed in J. H. Robinson, *Readings in European History* (1905), 72–73, is available online at the Fordham University Medieval Sourcebook: http://www.fordham.edu/halsall/source/gelasius1.html. See also Witte, "That Serpentine Wall of Separation," 1878–79.

57. Hyman, *Philosophy in the Middle Ages*, 716.

58. John Calvin, *Institutes of the Christian Religion*, Henry Beveridge, trans. (Grand Rapids: Eerdmans, 1979), 4.11.13. See also J.H. Merle d'Aubigné, *History of the Reformation in Europe in the Time of Calvin* (1880; photo. reprint 2000), 6:255–56 .

59. *See* Berman, *Law and Revolution*, 94–96; Cantor, *Civilization of the Middle Ages*, 87; Witte, "That Serpentine Wall of Separation," 1879–81.

60. For a Reformation-era telling of the story, by the Strasbourg reformer Martin Bucer, see Martin Bucer, *Concerning the True Care of Souls*, trans. Peter Beale, (Edinburgh: Banner of Truth, 2009), 153–55.

61. 1 C.W. Previté-Orton, *The Shorter Cambridge Medieval History* (Cambridge: Cambridge University Press 1962), 489–91.

62. Bucer, *Concerning the True Care of Souls*, 154.

63. Berman, *Law and Revolution*, 51.

64. See Karl Frederick Morrison, *The Two Kingdoms* (Princeton: Princeton University Press, 1964), 57.

65. Jaroslav Pelikan, *The Christian Tradition* (Chicago: University of Chicago Press, 1989), 5:322.

66. *Id.*

67. See Erwin Fahlbusch, et al., eds. *Encyclopedia of Christianity* (Grand Rapids: Eerdmans, 1999), 1:504. An adequate exploration of the recent Catholic scholarship on the subject of church, state, and specifically church autonomy, would take another book. For a sampling of the important recent scholarship, see Patrick McKinley Brennan, "Differentiating Church and State (Without Losing the Church)," *Georgetown Journal of Law & Government Policy* 7 (2009): 29 (a draft copy is available at SSRN: http://ssrn.com/abstract=1125441); Richard W. Garnett, "Church, State, and the Practice of Love," *Villanova Law Review* 52 (2007): 281, 293; Richard W. Garnett, "Pluralism, Dialogue, and Freedom: Professor Robert Rodes and the Church-State Nexus," *Journal of Law & Religion* 22 (2006-2007): 503, 521.

68. Titus, *God, Man, and Law*, 71.

69. Kenneth O. Morgan, *The Oxford Illustrated History of Britain* (Oxford: Oxford University Press, 2000), 125. At least, the king said something to that effect.

70. See Berman, *Law and Revolution*, 256; Arthur R. Hogue, *Origins of the Common Law* 38–44 (1966; reprint, Indianapolis: Liberty Fund, 1986); Paul Johnson, *The Offshore Islanders* (New York: Holt, Rinehart and Winston 1972), 98–99. See also Carl H. Esbeck, "Dissent and Disestablishment: The Church-State Settlement in the Early American Republic," *BYU Law Review* 2004:1385, 1405–07. The ecclesiastical privileges actually at issue between Becket and the king themselves presented a fascinating issue of church-state relations. For discussion, see below, chapter 10.

71. Edward Coke, "Second Part of the Institutes, Prologue," in *Selected Writings of Sir Edward Coke*, Steve Sheppard ed. (Indianapolis: Liberty Fund, 2003), 2:748.

72. See R.H. Helmholz, "**Magna** Carta and the ius commune," *University of Chicago Law Review* 66 (1999): 297, 313–314 (1999). See also discussion in Hosanna-Tabor Evangelical Lutheran Church and School v. Equal Employment Opportunity Commission, 132 S. Ct. 694, 702 (2012) ("The King in particular accepted the 'freedom of elections,' a right 'thought to be of the greatest necessity and importance to the English church.'").

73. Coke, "Second Part of the Institutes, Prologue," in *Selected Writings*, 747.

74. Hogue, *Origins of the Common Law*, 159.

75. Titus, *God, Man, and Law*, 71. "[N]ote that just as the lord pope has ordinary jurisdiction over all in spiritual matters, so the king has ordinary jurisdiction in his kingdom in temporal matters. . . . To the pope and the priesthood belong all things spiritual; to the king and kingdom those that are temporal . . . . Hence it is not within the province of the pope to dispose of temporal things or to order them, no more than may a king or prince deal with spiritual things, lest one put his sickle into the other's harvest. Just as the pope may ordain to orders and dignities in spiritual matters, so may the king in temporal, with respect to the giving of inheritances and the instituting of heirs . . . ." *Bracton on the Laws and Customs of England*, trans. Samuel E. Thorne, vol. 4:281, 298, from Bracton Online, Harvard Law School Library, http://hlsl5.law.harvard.edu/bracton/.

76. *Bracton on the Laws and Customs of England*, trans. Samuel E. Thorne, vol. 4:248, from Bracton Online, Harvard Law School Library, http://hlsl5.law.harvard.edu/bracton/.

77. Titus, 71. For more of the details of these jurisdictional controversies between common law courts and ecclesiastical courts, see Robert E. Rodes, *Lay Author-*

ity and Reformation in the English Church: Edward I to the Civil War (Notre Dame: University of Notre Dame Press, 1982), 12–49; R.H. Helmholz, *Roman Canon Law in Reformation England* (Cambridge: Cambridge University Press, 1990), 1-27.

CHAPTER 3

78.   See Philip Benedict, *Christ's Churches Purely Reformed: A Social History of Calvinism* (New Haven: Yale University Press, 2002). See also Robert M. Kingdon, "Calvin and Ecclesiastical Discipline," translated by David Hall from the original article in *Bulletin de la Societe de l'histoire du Protestantisme Francais, Janvier-Fevrier-Mars 2009* (Tome 155), 117-126. This translation of Kingdon's article is to be published with the papers presented at the Calvin 500 conference in Geneva, in press at the time of our first draft. We are indebted to David Hall for providing us with an advance copy.

79.   Quoted in Benedict, *Christ's Churches*, 22.

80.   Alister E. McGrath, *Reformation Thought: An Introduction*, 3d ed. (Oxford: Blackwell Publishers, 1999), 267.

81.   *Id.* at 265–67.

82.   John Witte, Jr., *Law and Protestantism* (Cambridge: Cambridge University Press, 2002), 6.

83.   Arthur P. Monahan, *From Personal Duties towards Personal Rights* (Montreal: McGill-Queen's University Press, 1994), 201.

84.   John R. Stumme and Robert W. Tuttle, "Lutheran Thinking on Church-State Issues," in John R. Stumme and Robert W. Tuttle, eds., *Church and State: Lutheran Perspectives* (Minneapolis: Fortress Press, 2003), 9.

85.   Stumme and Tuttle, *Church and State*, 9.

86.   In general, Luther was more hesitant and haphazard in fleshing out practical legal theory than were some of the other reformers. See John Eidsmoe, *God and Caesar* (Eugene, Oregon: Wipf & Stock, 1997), 14–15; Witte, *Law and Protestantism*, 10; Harold J. Berman, *Law and Revolution II* (Cambridge: Harvard University Press, 2003), 71–77. Luther's colleagues who were professional legal scholars invested more heavily in developing a Lutheran legal theory. See Witte, *Law and Protestantism*, 10.

87.   Duncan B. Forrester, "Martin Luther and John Calvin," in Leo Strauss and Joseph Cropsey, eds., *History of Political Philosophy* (Chicago: Rand McNally, 1963), 286–87.

88. See also See John Witte, Jr., "That Serpentine Wall of Separation," *Michigan Law Review* 101 (2003): 1883–1884.

89. Quoted in Naugle, *Worldview: The History of a Concept*, 16.

90. John Witte, Jr., *The Reformation of Rights* (Cambridge: Cambridge University Press, 2007), chapter 1.

91. Benedict, *Christ's Churches*, 82–84.

92. David W. Hall, *The Genevan Reformation and the American Founding* (Lanham, Maryland: Lexington, 2003); David W. Hall, *Calvin in the Public Square* (Phillipsburg, New Jersey: Presbyterian and Reformed, 2009); Douglas Kelly, *The Emergence of Liberty in the Modern World: The Influence of Calvin on Five Governments from the 16th Through 18th Centuries* (Philipsburg, New Jersey: Presbyterian and Reformed, 1992); John Witte, Jr., *The Reformation of Rights* (Cambridge: Cambridge University Press, 2007).

93. J.H. Merle d'Aubigné, *History of the Reformation in Europe in the Time of Calvin* (1880, photo. reprint 2000), 1:5.

94. Egbert Watson Smith, *The Creed of Presbyterians* (New York: Baker and Taylor, 1901), 119.

95. George Bancroft, *Literary and Historical Miscellanies* (New York: Harper and Brothers, 1855), 406.

96. John Adams, "Essay XIX," in *The Works of John Adams*, Charles Francis Adams, ed. (Boston, Little, Brown, 1851), 6:313–14.

97. *See* Benedict, *Christ's Churches*, 77–114. The notorious Servetus affair was, for instance, extremely complex. Calvin did testify against Servetus at the trial, but he did not pass the sentence, and when the city counsel sentenced Servetus to death at the stake, Calvin supported Servetus's plea for a more merciful means of execution. See Witte, *The Reformation of Rights*, 68.

98. The following summary of Calvin's relationship with Geneva is drawn primarily from Benedict, *Christ's Churches*, 77–114.

99. John Calvin, "Reply to Sadoleto," in John C. Olin, ed., *A Reformation Debate* (Grand Rapids: Baker, 1976), 80.

100. See John Calvin, *Institutes of the Christian Religion*, Henry Beveridge, trans. (Grand Rapids: Eerdmans, 1979), 4.11, 4.20. Unless noted otherwise, future quotations from Calvin's institutes are from this translation.

101. *Id.* at 4.20.1.

102. *Id.* at 4.11.1.

103. John Calvin, *Institutes of the Christian Religion,* J.T. McNeill, ed., F.L. Battles, trans. (1960; reprint, Louisville: Westminster John Knox, 2006), 4.20.1.

104. Joseph Morecraft III, "The Global Influence of John Calvin" (July 27, 2006) (unpublished paper, on file with Chalcedon Presbyterian Church, Cummings, Georgia), 3.

105. Calvin, *Institutes,* 4.11.5.

106. Calvin, *Institutes,* 4.11.3.

107. See Douglas Kelly, *The Emergence of Liberty in the Modern World: The Influence of Calvin on Five Governments from the 16th Through 18th Centuries* (Philipsburg, New Jersey: Presbyterian and Reformed, 1992), 139.

108. *Id.* at 15 (quoting John Calvin, letter of 24 October 1538).

109. Calvin, *Institutes,* 4.11.3.

110. See also Robert M. Kingdon, "Calvin and Ecclesiastical Discipline," translated by David Hall from the original article in *Bulletin de la Societe de l'histoire du Protestantisme Francais, Janvier-Fevrier-Mars 2009* (Tome 155), 117-126. This translation of Kingdon's article is to be published with the papers presented at the Calvin 500 conference in Geneva (in press). We are indebted to David Hall for providing us with an advance copy of the translation.

111. Willem van t' Spijker, "Bucer's Influence on Calvin," in D.F. Wright, ed., *Martin Bucer: Reforming Church and Community* (Cambridge: Cambridge University Press, 1994), 40. It is likely that Bucer influenced Calvin on the subject of discipline in particular; see Kingdon, "Calvin and Ecclesiastical Discipline," translated by David Hall from the original article in *Bulletin de la Societe de l'histoire du Protestantisme Francais, Janvier-Fevrier-Mars 2009* (Tome 155), 117-126.

112. Martin Greschat, "The Relation Between Church and Civil Community in Bucer's Reforming Work," in Wright, ed., *Martin Bucer,* 17, 24.

113. Willem van t' Spijker, "Bucer's Influence on Calvin," in Wright, ed., *Martin Bucer,* 41–42.

114. He was willing to allow significant amounts of state involvement in church affairs, more than Calvin or Viret would have been comfortable with. See Greschat, "The Relation Between Church and Civil Community in Bucer's Reforming Work," in Wright, ed., *Martin Bucer,* 20–22.

115. Martin Bucer, *Concerning the True Care of Souls,* trans. Peter Beale, (Edinburgh: Banner of Truth, 2009), 142.

116. He published more than forty books in his lifetime. Jean-Marc Berthoud, *Pierre Viret: A Forgotten Giant of the Reformation* (Tallahassee, Florida: Zurich,

2010)," unpublished manuscript (2008), 87–98.

117. Berthoud, *Pierre Viret*, 14–15.

118. J.A. Wylie, *The History of Protestantism* (1878).

119. Robert Linder, *The Political Ideas of Pierre Viret* (Geneva: Droz, 1964), 36.

120. Berthoud, *Pierre Viret*, 15.

121. Linder, *Political Ideas of Pierre Viret*, 35.

122. Linder, *Political Ideas of Pierre Viret*, 38–39.

123. Benedict, *Christ's Churches*, 148.

124. Benedict, *Christ's Churches*, 193.

CHAPTER 4

125. Philip Schaff, *History of the Christian Church* (New York, Scribner, 1888), 7:396–97.

126. 4 J.H. Merle d'Aubigné, *History of the Reformation in Europe in the Time of Calvin* (1880; photo. reprint 2000), 128.

127. Thomas Carlyle, *On Heroes, Hero-Worship, and the Heroic in History*, ed. Archibald MacMechan (Boston: Ginn and Company, 1901), 168.

128. *Southern Presbyterian Review*, July 1876, p. 442.

129. For a discussion on the date of Knox's birth, see Iain Murray, *A Scottish Christian Heritage* (Edinburgh: Banner of Truth, 2005), 8.

130. Thomas McCrie, *The Life of John Knox* (reprint, Milwaukee, OR: Back Home Industries, 2004), 276.

131. For a full discussion of the multiple assassination attempts on Wishart's life, see Jean Henri Merle d'Aubigné, *History of the Reformation in the Time of Calvin*, (Harrisonburg, VA, reprint 2000), 6:185–195.

132. John Knox , *History of the Reformation in Scotland* (Edinburgh: Banner of Truth, 2000), 56.

133. John Knox , *History of the Reformation in Scotland* (Edinburgh: Banner of Truth, 2000), 56–58.

134. Jean Henri Merle d'Aubigné, *History of the Reformation in the Time of Calvin*, 4 vols. (Harrisonburg, VA, reprint 2000), 4:207–14.

135. Douglas Wilson, *For Kirk and Covenant: The Stalwart Courage of John Knox*

(Nashville: Highland Books, 2000) pp. 22-23.

136. John Knox , *History of the Reformation in Scotland* (Edinburgh: Banner of Truth, 2000), 58–71.

137. *Ibid.*, p. 75.

138. Iain Murray, *A Scottish Christian Heritage* (Edinburgh: Banner of Truth Trust, 2005), 10–11. For information about Knox's release, see: John Knox , *History of the Reformation in Scotland*, pp. 60–61.

139. Thomas McCrie, *The Life of John Knox* (1814; reprint, Milwaukee, OR: Back Home Industries, 2004), 62–63.

140. *Ibid.*, pp. 63–68.

141. For a detailed account of Knox's ministry in England, see Peter Lorimer, *John Knox and the Church of England: His Work in Her Pulpit and His Influence on Her Liturgy, Articles, and Parties* (London: Henry S. King, 1875).

142. The Scottish Parliament ratified the Confession of Faith; the Book of Discipline became embroiled in controversy over the method of financing the church and was never ratified. The controversial proposal recommended that all lands that belonged to the Roman Catholic Church should be turned over to the Reformed church for its use. L. Anthony Curto, "John Knox: The Watchman of Scotland" http://www.reformed.org/webfiles/antithesis/index. html?mainframe=/webfiles/antithesis/v1n3/ant_v1n3_knox.html.

143. W. Stanford Reid, *The Trumpeter of God* (Grand Rapids: Baker Book House, 1982), 207.

144. Scottish Confession of Faith, 3.18.

145. Quoted in Michael F. Graham, *The Uses of Reform: Godly Discipline and Popular Behavior in Scotland and Beyond, 1560–1610* (Leiden: E.J. Brill, 1996), 41. See also W.M. Heatherington, *History of the Church of Scotland* (New York: Robert Carter, 1860), 56.

146. See Douglas Kelly, *The Emergence of Liberty in the Modern World: The Influence of Calvin on Five Governments from the 16th Through 18th Centuries* (Philipsburg, New Jersey: Presbyterian and Reformed, 1992), 56–64.

147. *Id.* at 65.

148. *See id.* at 64–65.

149. Thomas McCrie, *The Life of Andrew Melville*, 2d ed. (Edinburgh: William Blackwell, 1824), 1:119–20.

150. Kelly, *The Emergence of Liberty*, 66 (quoting James Kirk, *The Second Book of*

Discipline (1980), 58)).

151. Justo L. Gonzalez, *Essential Theological Terms* (Louisville: Westminster John Knox, 2005), 54.

152. David C. Lachman, "Preface to the Reprint," George Gillespie, *Aaron's Rod Blossoming* (1646; reprint, Harrisonburg, Virginia: Sprinkle, 1985).

153. Thomas McCrie, *The Story of the Scottish Church* (1875; photo. reprint 1988), 84.

154. *Id.* at 85.

155. Philip Benedict, *Christ's Churches Purely Reformed: A Social History of Calvinism* (New Haven: Yale University Press, 2002), 385.

156. Rutherford is an important political theorist mostly remembered as the author of *Lex Rex* (1644), arguing that the king is under the law, and thus providing a rationale for resistance. See David W. Hall, *The Genevan Reformation and the American Founding* (Lanham, Maryland: Lexington, 2003), 252–54.

157. Alexander Henderson et al, *The Protestation of the General Assembly of the Church of Scotland...Subscribers of the Covenant lately Renewed* (Glasgow, Scotland, November 1638). The dispute with the king led to the outbreak of the Bishops' Wars between Royalists and Covenanters, and eventually between the king and the Puritan Parliament of England.

158. H.C.G. Matthew & Brian Harrison, eds., *Oxford Dictionary of National Biography* (2004), 22:257.

159. This state-above-the-church view may have been typically English, but throughout his book, Gillespie referred to it as Erastianism. See Lachman, "Preface to the Reprint" of Gillespie, *Aaron's Rod Blossoming*.

160. Gillespie, *Aaron's Rod*, xvi.

161. *Id.* at 3. *See also* Daniel J. Ford, *In the Name of God, Amen* (St. Louis: Lex Rex, 2003), 229.

162. "Grand Remonstrance," November 6, 1641, quoted in Joseph C. Morecraft III, *Authentic Christianity: An Exposition of the Theology and Ethics of the Westminster Larger Catechism* (Atlanta: American Vision, 2009), 37.

163. W.M. Hetherington, *History of the Westminster Assembly of Divines*, ed. Robert Williamson, 4th ed. (Edinburgh: James Gemmell, 1878), 235.

164. Benedict, *Christ's Churches*, 400–01; see also Hetherington, *History of the Westminster Assembly of Divines*, 432–74.

165. Westminster Confession XXIII, 1, 3 (1646)

166. Iain Murray, "Richard Baxter—'The Reluctant Puritan'?," in *Advancing in*

Adversity (Westminster Conference 1991), 1.

167. "An Admonition to the Parliament," 1572, in W.H. Frere, ed., *Puritan Manifestoes* (London: SPCK, 1907), 30.

168. For the story of this document and the ensuing confrontation at the Hampton Court Conference, see Benson Bobrick, *Wide as the Waters* (New York: Penguin, 2001), 202–214.

169. Henry Gee and William John Hardy, ed., *Documents Illustrative of English Church History* (New York: Macmillan, 1896), 510, and available online at http://history.hanover.edu/texts/ENGref/er88.html.

170. Quoted in Benson Bobrick, *Wide as the Waters* (New York: Penguin, 2001), 212.

171. For example, these issues of exercise of proper jurisdictional power and stopping abuses of church discipline came up again, though in a different context, in the important "Root and Branch Petition," December 11, 1640, para. 25, *in* Samuel Rawson Gardiner, ed., *The Constitutional Documents of the Puritan Revolution, 1625–1660* (3rd ed., Oxford: Oxford University Press, 1906), 142.

172. Lynell Friese "The Work and Thought of Richard Baxter," http://www.thirdmill.org/files/english/html/ch/CH.h.Friesen.Baxter.2.html (last visited September 4, 2007).

173. Richard Baxter, *A Holy Commonwealth*, William Lamont, ed. (Cambridge: Cambridge University Press, 1994), 130, 131–32.

CHAPTER 5

174. See John Witte, Jr., *The Reformation of Rights* (Cambridge: Cambridge University Press, 2007), chapter 5.

175. See Sanford Kessler, "Tocqueville's Puritans: Christianity and the American Founding," *Journal of Politics* 54 (1992): 776.

176. William Bradford, *Of Plymouth Plantation*, Samuel Elliot Morison, ed. (New York: Modern Library, 1967), 10.

177. Daniel J. Ford, *In the Name of God, Amen* (St. Louis: Lex Rex, 2003), 230.

178. James H. Hutson, *Religion and the Founding of the American Republic* (Washington, D.C.: Library of Congress, 1998), 5, 7.

179. Massachusetts Body of Liberties (1641), para. 58, in *Old South Leaflets* (Boston: Directors of the Old South Work), 7:268, online at http://history.hanover.edu/texts/masslib.html.

180. John Cotton, *The Way of the Churches of Christ in New England* (London, 1645), 19.

181. Francis J. Bremer, *First Founders: American Puritans and Puritanism in an Atlantic World* (University of New Hampshire Press, 2012), 54.

182. The full title is: *The Cambridge Platform: A Platform of Church Discipline Gathered Out of the Word of God; and agreed upon by the Elders and Messengers of the Churches Assembled in the Synod at Cambridge in New England to be presented to the Churches and General Court for their consideration and acceptance in the Lord.*

183. Daniel Dreisbach and Mark David Hall, *The Sacred Rights of Conscience: Selected Readings on Religious Liberty and Church-State Relations in the American Founding* (Indianapolis: Liberty Fund, 2009), 165.

184. Ibid, 168.

185. Ibid, 172.

186. Some historians don't think that that the New England Puritans should get credit for separating church and state because the Puritans still expected the civil magistrate to have a role in reinforcing the church. See, for example, Philip Hamburger, *Separation of Church and State* (Cambridge: Harvard University Press, 2002), 80. But this confuses two issues. One issue is whether the church and the state are separate institutions. The other issue is what role the state has when it interacts with the church and vice versa. It is possible for the Puritans to recognize the jurisdictional and institutional separation, on the one hand, while on the other hand, endorsing closer interactions between church and state than we are accustomed to in modern America. See John Witte, Jr., "That Serpentine Wall of Separation," *Michigan Law Review* 101 (2003): 1887–1889.

187. Ford, *In the Name of God, Amen*, 231.

188. Even in Virginia, the influence of Puritan Calvinism was prevalent among the clergy. See Perry Miller, "The Religious Impulse in the Founding of Virginia: Religion and Society in the Early Literature," *William and Mary Quarterly* 5 (1948): 492, 499–503, and Hutson, *Religion and the Founding of the American Republic*, 17–18. In fact, John Rolfe quoted Calvin's *Institutes* to the governor when explaining his reasons for seeking to marry the native princess, Pocahontas. See Rolfe to Sir Thomas Dale, in Edward Wright Hale, ed., *Jamestown Narratives* (Round House, 1998), 854 n. 3.

189. See Michael W. McConnell, "Establishment and Disestablishment at the Founding, Part I: Establishment of Religion," *William & Mary Law Review* (2003): 2105–2208.

190. *See generally* Bernard Bailyn, *Voyagers to the West: A Passage in the Peopling of*

America on the Eve of the Revolution (New York: Knopf, 1986). We are grateful to Joseph Morecraft for pointing us to this history.

191. *Id.* at 78–79.

192. *Id.* at 90–91.

193. Bailyn, *Voyagers to the West*, 26.

194. Bailyn, *Voyagers to the West*, 26.

195. John Eidsmoe, *Christianity and the Constitution* (Grand Rapids: Baker, 1987), 19.

196. David W. Hall, *The Genevan Reformation and the American Founding* (Lanham, Maryland: Lexington, 2003), 417.

197. Eidsmoe, *Christianity and the Constitution*, 19.

198. See Martha Lou Lemmon Stohlman, *John Witherspoon: Parson, Politician, Patriot* (Philadelphia: Westminster Press, 1976), 19; Varnum Lansing Collins, *President Witherspoon*, 2 vols. (Princeton: Princeton University Press, 1925), 1:5–7.

199. L.H. Butterfield, ed., *John Witherspoon Comes to America* (Princeton: Princeton University Library, 1953), xii–xiii; also see Stohlman, chapter 3.

200. For general analysis of Witherspoon's theology and its influence on his political positions, see Roger Schultz, "Covenanting in America: The Political Theology of John Witherspoon," *Journal of Christian Reconstruction* 12 (1988): 179, and Gideon Mailer, "Anglo-Scottish Union and John Witherspoon's American Revolution," *William and Mary Quarterly* 67 (2010): 709–746.

201. See Stohlman, 172; Mary-Elaine Swanson, *The Education of James Madison* (Montgomery, Alabama: Hoffman Education Center, 1992).

202. Witherspoon was the head of the national Presbyterian church. See Jeffry H. Morrison, *John Witherspoon and the Founding of the American Republic* (Notre Dame: University of Notre Dame Press, 2005), 6.

203. Westminster Confession (1647), XXIII, 3, "Of the Civil Magistrate."

204. Westminster Confession (1647), XXIII, 3, "Of the Civil Magistrate."

205. *Id.*

206. A reference to Isaiah 49:23: "And kings shall be thy nursing fathers, and their queens thy nursing mothers . . . ." This passage was frequently cited in Reformed descriptions of church and state for its implication that the civil magistrates should provide a friendly societal environment for the church to prosper in. See, *e.g.*, Frank Lambert, *The Founding Fathers and the Place of Religion in*

America (Princeton: Princeton University Press, 2003), 48; James H. Hutson, *Church and State in America: The First Two Centuries* (Cambridge: Cambridge University Press, 2008), 8.

207. Westminster Confession (1789), XXIII.3, "Of the Civil Magistrate."

208. Morrison, *John Witherspoon and the Founding of the American Republic*, 109.

209. Quoted in L. Gordon Tait, *The Piety of John Witherspoon: Pew, Pulpit, and Public Forum* (Louisville: Geneva Press, 2001), 20.

210. See Michael W. McConnell, "The Origins and Historical Understanding of Free Exercise of Religion," *Harvard Law Review* 103 (1990): 1409, 1436–1443. Still, it would be several decades before all states disestablished their state churches. Following independence, "six states either upheld religious establishments in practice . . . or had constitutional provisions permitting non-preferential establishment." McConnell, "Establishment and Disestablishment at the Founding, Part I: Establishment of Religion," 1019–1020. Eventually, though, many states passed their own establishment clause analogues. G. Alan Tarr, "Church and State in the States," *Washington Law Review* 64 (1989): 73; see also Steven G. Calabresi and Sarah E. Agudo, "Individual Rights Under State Constitutions when the Fourteenth Amendment Was Ratified in 1868: What Rights Are Deeply Rooted in American History and Tradition?," *Texas Law Review* 87 (2008): 7, 31–33.

211. See Carl H. Esbeck, "Protestant Dissent and the Virginia Disestablishment, 1776-1786," *Georgetown Journal of Law & Public Policy* 7 (2009): 51; Hutson, *Religion and the Founding*, 66.

212. The contributions of the Baptists to religious liberty in Virginia are extensive; *see* Charles Fenton James, *Documentary History of the Struggle for Religious Liberty in Virginia* (Lynchburg, Virginia: J.P. Bell, 1899); Philip Hamburger, *Separation of Church and State* (Cambridge: Harvard University Press, 2002), 92. On their tradition of religious freedom, James has written,

> Of the Baptist, at least, it may be truly said that they entered the conflict in the New World with a clear and consistent record on the subject of soul liberty. "Freedom of conscience" had ever been one of their fundamental tenets. John Locke, in his "Essay on Toleration," says: "The Baptist were the first and only propounders of absolute liberty, just and true liberty, equal and impartial liberty." And the great American historian, Bancroft, says: "Freedom of conscience, unlimited freedom of mind, was from the first a trophy of the Baptist."

Id. at 14. Thomas Jefferson used the phrase, "separation of church and state," in a letter to a Baptist organization. He was assuring them that the federal government would not create a religious establishment that would infringe on their freedom of religion. See Daniel L. Dreisbach, *Thomas Jefferson and the Wall of Separation between Church and State* (New York: New York University Press, 2002).

213. See Esbeck, "Protestant Dissent and the Virginia Disestablishment, 1776-1786," 51.

214. Hutson, *Religion and the Founding*, 66–74; Hamburger, *Separation of Church and State*, 103–105; Esbeck, "Protestant Dissent and the Virginia Disestablishment, 1776-1786," 51; Carl H. Esbeck, "Dissent and Disestablishment: The Church-State Settlement in the Early American Republic," *BYU Law Review* 2004:1385, 1498.

215. James Madison, "Memorial and Remonstrance Against Religious Assessments" (1785), in Charles S. Hyneman and Donald S. Lutz, eds., *American Political Writing During the Founding Era* (Indianapolis: Liberty Press, 1983), 1:632.

216. *Id.*

217. *Id.*

218. *Id.* at 634.

219. *See* John Witte, Jr., *Law and Protestantism* (Cambridge: Cambridge University Press, 2002), 6 on the Reformation view ("no person and no institution obstructed or mediated by any other in relationship to and accountability before God."), which sounds very much like Madison's argument.

220. *See* Esbeck, "Dissent and Disestablishment," 1560.

221. Forrest McDonald, *E Pluribus Unum* (Boston: Houghton Mifflin, 1965) 316–17; Thomas B. McAffee, "The Federal System as Bill of Rights: Original Understandings, Modern Misreadings," *Villanova Law Review* 43 (1998): 17, 77–97.

222. Douglas G. Smith, "The Establishment Clause: Corollary of Eighteenth-Century Corporate Law?," *Northwestern University Law Review* 98 (2003): 239, 271–72; McAffee, "The Federal System as Bill of Rights," 94.

223. Akhil Reed Amar, "The Bill of Rights as a Constitution," *Yale Law Journal* 100 (1991): 1131; McAffee, "The Federal System as Bill of Rights," 77–97; McDonald, *E Pluribus Unum*, 351–52, 367. See also the historical summary in Wallace v. Jaffree, 472 U.S. 38, 91–114 (Rehnquist, J., dissenting).

224. Hutson, *Religion and the Founding*, 78–79.

225. See Hamburger, *Separation of Church and State*, 89–107. See also Witte, "That

Serpentine Wall of Separation," 1891–1892; Michael W. McConnell, "Reflections on *Hosanna-Tabor*," *Harvard Journal of Law and Public Policy* 35 (2012): 821, 828.

226. See Hutson, 79–80.

227. As legal scholar Carl Esbeck succinctly stated, "The First Amendment . . . is a recognition . . . that the civil courts have no subject matter jurisdiction over the internal affairs of religious organizations." Esbeck, "Dissent and Disestablishment," 1589. The U.S. Supreme Court also recently noted:

> By forbidding the "establishment of religion" and guaranteeing the "free exercise thereof," the Religion Clauses ensured that the new Federal Government—unlike the English Crown—would have no role in filling ecclesiastical offices. The Establishment Clause prevents the Government from appointing ministers, and the Free Exercise Clause prevents it from interfering with the freedom of religious groups to select their own.

Hosanna-Tabor Evangelical Lutheran Church and School v. Equal Employment Opportunity Commission, 132 S. Ct. 694, 703 (2012).

228. Indeed, just as Calvin would have wanted, the first constitutional Congress kept itself out of church affairs while openly displaying its theological beliefs as it moved for a day of thanksgiving and then proceeded to attend church on that occasion.

229. Michael W. McConnell, "Religion and Constitutional Rights: Why is Religious Liberty the 'First Freedom'?," *Cardozo Law Review* 21 (2000): 1246.

CHAPTER 6

230. Westbrook v. Penley, 231 S.W.3d 389, 391 (Tex. 2007) (quoting C.L. Penley, letter of 7 November 2001).

231. *Id.*

232. Originally, the suit was against Westbrook as well as the church elders and the church itself, alleging defamation, breach of fiduciary duty, intentional infliction of emotional distress, invasion of privacy, and professional negligence in his role as a marriage counselor. Subsequently, all claims were dismissed except the professional negligence claim against Westbrook himself.

233. *Westbrook,* 231 S.W.3d at 397.

234. *Westbrook,* 231 S.W.3d at 398, *quoting* Minton v. Leavell, 297 S.W. 615, 621-22

(Tex. Civ. App. 1927).

235. Bryce v. Episcopal Church in the Diocese of Colorado, 289 F.3d 648, 655 (10th Cir. 2002), *citing* Kedroff v. St. Nicholas Cathedral of Russian Orthodox Church, 344 U.S. 94, 116–17 (1952).

236. Watson v. Jones, 80 U.S. 679, 727 (1872).

237. Kedroff v. St. Nicholas Cathedral of Russian Orthodox Church, 344 U.S. 94 (1952).

238. Hosanna-Tabor Evangelical Lutheran Church and School v. Equal Employment Opportunity Commission, 132 S. Ct. 694, 702 (2012).

239. See *Hosanna-Tabor*, 132 S. Ct. 694, 702; *Bryce*, 289 F.3d at 655; Ayon v. Gourley, 47 F. Supp. 2d 1246, 1249–50 (D. Colo. 1998), *aff'd*, 185 F.3d 873 (10th Cir. 1999). See generally Scott C. Idleman, "Tort Liability, Religious Entities, and the Decline of Constitutional Protection," *Indiana Law Journal* 75 (2000): 219, 223–25. Interestingly, church autonomy doctrine was first articulated *before* its constitutional basis was identified. Watson v. Jones, 80 U.S. 679 (1872), the first autonomy case in the Supreme Court, nowhere mentions a constitutional basis for its holding. *See Kedroff*, 344 U.S. at 115. This suggests that church autonomy doctrine grew out of a larger, broader theoretical tradition that shared a common source with the First Amendment. Hence, church autonomy can be found in the First Amendment, but it did not originate there. In light of the history outlined above, the theological "two kingdoms" concept must be considered a primary influence.

240. *See, e.g., Kedroff*, 344 U.S. at 119; Westbrook v. Penley, 231 S.W.3d 389, 397 n. 6 (Tex. 2007).

241. *Westbrook*, 231 S.W.3d 389, 395 (Tex. 2007), *quoting* Lemon v. Kurtzman, 403 U.S. 602, 614 (1971), and Aguilar v. Felton, 473 U.S. 402, 410, (1985) (*quoting* McCollum v. Bd. of Ed., 333 U.S. 203, 212, (1948)).

242. Abraham Kuyper, *Lectures on Calvinism* (Grand Rapids: Eerdmans, 1943).

243. "The right to organize voluntary religious associations to assist in the expression and dissemination of any religious doctrine, and to create tribunals for the decision of controverted questions of faith within the association, and for the ecclesiastical government of all the individual members, congregations, and officers within the general association, is unquestioned." *Watson*, 80 U.S. at 728.

244. Kedroff v. St. Nicholas Cathedral, 344 U.S. 94, 116 (1952).

245. *Westbrook*, 231 S.W.3d 389, 397 (Tex. 2007), *citing* Kedroff v. St. Nicholas Cathedral, 344 U.S. 94, 116 (1952).

246. *Watson*, 80 U.S. at 728–29. Another, even earlier, case stated a similar rationale:

"Amongst these powers and privileges [of churches], established by long and immemorial usage, churches have authority to deal with their members, for immoral and scandalous conduct; and for that purpose, to hear complaints, to take evidence and to decide; and, upon conviction, to administer proper punishment by way of rebuke, censure, suspension and excommunication. To this jurisdiction, every member, by entering into the church covenant, submits, and is bound by his consent." Farnsworth v. Storrs, 59 Mass. 412, 415–16 (1850).

247. Yates v. El Bethel Primitive Baptist Church, 847 So. 2d 331, 355 (Ala. 2002) (Moore, C.J., dissenting).

248. *Watson,* 80 U.S. at 731.

249. *Id.* at 729.

250. See, for a negative example, Guinn v. Church of Christ of Collinsville, 775 P.2d 766 (Okla. 1989). See discussion in H. Wayne House, *Christian Ministries and the Law* (rev. ed., Grand Rapids: Kregel, 1999), 69–72.

251. Abyssinia Missionary Baptist Church v. Nixon, 340 So. 2d 746 (Ala. 1977); Yates v. El Bethel Primitive Baptist Church, 847 So. 2d 331 (Ala. 2002).

252. *Abyssinia,* 340 So. 2d at 748.

253. *Yates,* 847 So. 2d at 356–57 (Moore, C.J., dissenting) (emphasis in original) (quoting Watson v. Jones, 80 U.S. 679, 730 (1872)).

254. *See* Harris v. Matthews, 643 S.E.2d 566 (N.C. 2007). *See also* Bryce v. Episcopal Church in the Diocese of Colorado, 289 F.3d 648, 654 (10th Cir. 2002).

255. *Hosanna-Tabor,* 132 S. Ct. at 709 n. 4.

256. What lawyers call an "affirmative" defense.

257. *See, e.g.,* Malichi v. Archdiocese of Miami, 945 So. 2d 526 (Fla. App. 2006).

258. *See, e.g.,* Dobrata v. Free Serbian Orthodox Church "St. Nicholas," 952 P.2d 1190 (Ariz. App. 1998) ("a civil court cannot . . . decide a dispute between a church and its priest concerning the church's termination of a priest's employment"); Abrams v. Watchtower Bible & Tract Soc'y of N.Y., 715 N.E.2d 798 (Ill. App. 1999) (suit barred where resolution would require "[c]ivil court review of . . . ecclesiastic and religious decisions"); Mallette v. Church of God Int'l, 789 So. 2d 120 (Miss. App. 2001) ("the disciplining of a minister is church-related and the doctrine of ecclesiastical abstention requires us to abstain from questioning the matter of Mallette's discipline"); Archdiocese of Miami, Inc., v. Minagorri, 954 So. 2d 640 (Fla. App. 2007) ("the 'ecclesiastical abstention doctrine,' precludes courts from exercising jurisdiction where an employment decision concerns a member of the clergy or an employee in a ministerial position"); Southeastern Conf. Ass'n of Seventh-Day Adventists, Inc. v. Dennis, 862

So. 2d 842 (Fla. App. 2003) ("[c]ourts may not consider employment disputes between a religious organization and its clergy" when involving "questions of internal church discipline, faith, and organization that are governed by ecclesiastical rule, custom, and law").

259. *See* Marjorie A. Shields, Annotation, "Construction and Application of Church Autonomy Doctrine," 123 A.L.R. 5th 385 (2004). In 1981, constitutional law scholar Douglas Laycock used the term in an influential article on the religion clauses: Douglas Laycock, "Towards a General Theory of the Religion Clauses: The Case of Church Labor Relations and the Right to Church Autonomy," *Columbia Law Review* 81 (1981): 1373. Since then, "autonomy" has swept through the case law. The Texas Supreme Court adopted the autonomy term in a recent, carefully-reasoned opinion, an apparently self-conscious choice— for the implications of the term had been discussed in an important amicus brief before the court. Brief for National Association of Evangelicals as Amici Curiae Supporting Petitioner, 4–5, Westbrook v. Penley, 231 S.W.3d 389 (Tex. 2007), 2006 WL 2843840. In the *Hosanna-Tabor* case, the U.S. Supreme Court dealt with a particular application of the church autonomy principle in the context of federal antidiscrimination law, an application that has long had a name of its own: the "ministerial exception." The Court stuck with this term, which is something of a term of art in the field of antidiscrimination law. Still, the terminology of "autonomy" managed to make its way into the concurring opinions of Justice Thomas and Justice Alito (both wrote about "religious autonomy"). See *Hosanna-Tabor*, 132 U.S. at 710 (Thomas, J., concurring); *Hosanna-Tabor*, 132 U.S. at 711–12, 715 (Alito, J., concurring).

260. Westbrook v. Penley, 231 S.W.3d 389, 395 (Tex. 2007).

CHAPTER 7

261. Biblical sanctions should not be primarily thought of as punitive in purpose, but rather as restorative. This is explained in more detail in chapter 9.

262. "[I]f we would not make void the promise of the keys, and abolish altogether excommunication, solemn admonitions, and everything of that description, we must, of necessity, give some jurisdiction to the Church. . . . This Christ establishes in his Church . . . and with a heavy sanction." John Calvin, *Institutes of the Christian Religion*, Henry Beveridge, trans. (Grand Rapids: Eerdmans, 1979), 4.11.3. Unless noted otherwise, future quotations from Calvin's institutes are from this translation.

263. *See, e.g.*, Westminster Confession of Faith XXIII, III (1646); Westminster Shorter Catechism XXXI, II (1647); Heidelberg Catechism 83, 85 (1563). See

also the discussion later in this book in chapters 9 and 10.

264. Calvin, *Institutes*, 4.11.5.

265. *Id.*

266. Farnsworth v. Storrs, 59 Mass. 412, 416 (1850).

267. Westbrook v. Penley, 231 S.W.3d 389 (Tex. 2007)

268. *Westbrook*, 231 S.W.3d at 398, *quoting* Minton v. Leavell, 297 S.W. 615, 621-22 (Tex. Civ. App. 1927).

269. Serbian Eastern Orthodox Diocese for U. S. of America and Canada v. Milivojevich, 426 U.S. 696 (1976).

270. *Id.* at 709.

271. *See, e.g.*, Andrew Soukup, "Note, Reformulating Church Autonomy: How *Employment Division v. Smith* Provides a Framework for Fixing the Neutral Principles Approach," *Notre Dame Law Review* 82 (2007): 1679, 1688–92 (2007); Marci A. Hamilton, "Religious Institutions, the No-Harm Doctrine, and the Public Good," *BYU Law Review* 2004: 1099, 1162.

272. Though there still may be some confusing and arguably inconsistent statements in the Court's opinions. Michael William Galligan, "Note, Judicial Resolution of Intrachurch Disputes," *Columbia Law Review* 83 (1983): 2007, 2016.

273. Jones v. Wolf, 443 U.S. 595, 604 (1979), *citing* Serbian Eastern Orthodox Diocese for U. S. of America and Canada v. Milivojevich, 426 U.S. 696, 709 (1976).

274. Watson v. Jones, 80 U.S. 679, 731 (1872).

275. *See Serbian Eastern Orthodox*, 426 U.S. at 708–12.

276. It is important to note that, when the courts use the term "neutral" in this context, they are speaking in relation to the specific doctrinal *issue* under discussion. This is not to be confused with the concept of philosophical or religious "neutrality," which has been (rightly) criticized by philosophers and theologians. Greg L. Bahnsen, *Van Til's Apologetic* (Phillipsburg: Presbyterian and Reformed, 1998), 101–02, 127–28, 145–54; Roy A. Clouser, *The Myth of Religious Neutrality*, rev. ed. (Notre Dame: University of Notre Dame Press, 2005).

277. Calvin, *Institutes*, 4.11.5.

278. In recent years, courts across the country have recognized and applied the church autonomy doctrine numerous times. See, for example, decisions from Colorado (Seefried v. Hummel, 148 P.3d 184 (Colo. App. 2005)), Connecticut (Rweyemamu v. Commission on Human Rights & Opportunities, 911 A.2d 319 (Conn. App. 2006)), Florida (Southeastern Conf. Ass'n of Seventh-Day

Adventists, Inc. v. Dennis, 862 So. 2d 842 (Fla. App. 2003); Malichi v. Arch-diocese of Miami, 945 So. 2d 526 (Fla. App. 2006)), Indiana (Brazauskas v. Fort Wayne-South Bend Diocese, Inc., 796 N.E.2d 286 (In. 2003), *cert. denied*, 541 U.S. 902 (2004)), Maryland (Montrose Christian School Corp. v. Walsh, 770 A.2d 111 (Md. App. 2001)), Massachusetts (Hiles v. Episcopal Diocese of Massachusetts, 773 N.E.2d 929 (Mass. 2002)), Mississippi (Mallette v. Church of God Int'l, 789 So. 2d 120 (Miss. App. 2001)), Missouri (Rolfe v. Parker, 968 S.W.2d 178 (Mo. App. 1998)), New Jersey (Solid Rock Baptist Church v. Carlton, 789 A.2d 149 (N.J. Super. 2002)), New Mexico (Celnik v. Congrega-tion B'nai Israel, 131 P.3d 102 (N.M. App. 2006)), Rhode Island (Heroux v. Carpentier, 1998 WL 388298 (R.I. Super. Ct. 1998)), Tennessee (Anderson v. Watchtower Bible & Tract Soc'y of N.Y., Inc., 2007 Tenn. App. LEXIS 29 (Tenn. App. 2007)), Texas (Westbrook v. Penley, 231 S.W.3d 389 (Tex. 2007)), North Carolina (Harris v. Matthews, 643 S.E.2d 566, 273 (N.C. 2007)).

279. For defamation cases, consider for example: Paul v. Watchtower Bible & Tract Soc., 819 F.2d 875 (9th Cir. 1987); Hiles v. Episcopal Diocese of Massachu-setts, 773 N.E.2d 929 (Mass. 2002); Seefried v. Hummel, 148 P.3d 184 (Colo. App. 2005).

280. Dolquist v. Heartland Presbytery, 2004 WL 74318 (D. Kan. 2004).

281. Heroux v. Carpentier, 1998 WL 388298 (R.I. Super. Ct. 1998).

282. For examples: Brazauskas v. Fort Wayne-South Bend Diocese, Inc., 796 N.E.2d 286 (2003), *cert. denied*, cert. denied, 541 U.S. 902 (2004) (claims of interference with business relationship); Westbrook v. Penley, 231 S.W.3d 389 (Tex. 2007) (claims of professional negligence); Brazauskas v. Fort Wayne-South Bend Diocese, Inc., 796 N.E.2d 286 (In. 2003), *cert. denied*, 541 U.S. 902 (2004) (claim of "blacklisting"); Gabriel v. Immanuel Evangelical Lutheran Church, Inc., 640 N.E.2d 681 (Ill. App. Ct. 1994) (claim of breach of contract); Paul v. Watchtower Bible & Tract Soc., 819 F.2d 875 (9th Cir. 1987) (claim of invasion of privacy).

283. *See, e.g.,* EEOC v. Roman Catholic Diocese, 213 F.3d 795, 800 (4th Cir. 2000); EEOC v. Southwestern Baptist Theological Seminary, 651 F.2d 277 (5th Cir. 1981); Gellington v. Christian Methodist Episcopal Church, 203 F.3d 1299 (11th Cir. 2000); Bollard v. California Province of the Soc'y of Jesus, 196 F.3d 940 (9th Cir. 2000); Werft v. Desert Southwest Annual Conf., 377 F.3d 1099 (9th Cir. 2004); EEOC v. Catholic Univ. of Am., 83 F.3d 455 (D.C. Cir. 1996); Young v. Northern Ill. Conference of United Methodist Church, 21 F.3d 184 (7th Cir. 1994); Scharon v. St. Luke's Episcopal Presbyterian Hosp., 929 F.2d 360 (8th Cir. 1991); Rockwell v. Roman Catholic Archdiocese, 2002 U.S. Dist. LEXIS 20992 (3rd Cir. 2002).

284. Gabriel v. Immanuel Evangelical Lutheran Church, Inc., 640 N.E.2d 681 (Ill. App. Ct. 1994).

285. Flax v. Reconstructionist Rabbinical College, 44 Pa. D. & C.3d 435 (C.P. 1987), *aff'd*, 538 A.2d 947 (Pa. Super. Ct. 1987).

286. *Westbrook*, 231 S.W.3d at 397

287. William Strong, *Two Lectures upon the Relations of Civil Law to Church Polity, Discipline, and Property* (New York: Dodd and Mead, 1875), 38–39. Associate Justice William Strong served on the U.S. Supreme court from 1870–80. From 1866 to 1869, he was president of the National Reform Association, which since 1864 called for an amendment to the United States Constitution confessing Jesus Christ as King of the nation. He opposed a national church.

288. Calvin, *Institutes*, 4.11.5.

289. Watson v. Jones, 80 U.S. 679, 727 (1872).

290. Gonzalez v. Roman Catholic Archbishop, 280 U.S. 1, 16 (1929).

291. Kedroff v. St. Nicholas Cathedral, 344 U.S. 94, 116 (1952).

292. Solid Rock Baptist Church v. Carlton, 789 A.2d 149, 153 (N.J. Super. 2002).

293. *Id.* at 160.

294. Harris v. Matthews, 643 S.E.2d 566, 571 (N.C. 2007).

295. Presbyterian Church v. Hull Church, 393 U.S. 440 (1969). But an argument can be made that courts can enforce property trusts that involve doctrine, so long as the only question is a *factual* question ("has doctrine in fact changed?") rather than a normative question ("has this church followed correct doctrine?"). See Justin M. Gardner, Note, Ecclesiastical Divorce in Hierarchical Denominations and the Resulting Custody Battle Over Church Property: How the Supreme Court Has Needlessly Rendered Church Property Trusts Ineffectual, 6 *Ave Maria Law Review* 235 (2007).

296. Bryce v. Episcopal Church in the Diocese of Colorado, 289 F.3d 648 (10th Cir. 2002).

297. *Hosanna Tabor*, 132 S. Ct. at 706.

298. *Hosanna Tabor*, 132 S. Ct. at 709 (internal citation omitted).

CHAPTER 8

299. Christopher Hitchens, Bring the Pope to Justice, Newsweek April 23, 2010, (issue of May 3, 2010), http://www.newsweek.com/id/236934.

300. Harold J. Berman, *Law and Revolution* (Cambridge: Harvard University Press, 1983), 260–64.

301. *Id.* at 261. The ecclesiastical canon law also provided that the ecclesiastical courts had jurisdiction, not just over criminal matters, but over all civil suits involving the clergy. The state, in other words, had no jurisdiction over the persons of the clergy. In England, though, the canon law rule on civil suits was for the most part ignored—suits involving clergy were generally brought in the common law courts. Becket's fight was solely on the issue of felony criminal jurisdiction. See R.H. Helmholz, *Roman Canon Law in Reformation England* (Cambridge: Cambridge University Press, 1990), 9–11; Robert E. Rodes, *Lay Authority and Reformation in the English Church: Edward I to the Civil War* (Notre Dame: University of Notre Dame Press, 1982), 31, 33–34.

302. *See* Rollin M. Perkins & Ronald N. Boyce, *Criminal Law*, 3rd ed. (Mineola, New York: Foundation Press, 1982), 4–5, 1020; Robert E. Rodes, *Lay Authority and Reformation in the English Church: Edward I to the Civil War* (Notre Dame: University of Notre Dame Press, 1982), 31–33; Phillip M. Spector, "The Sentencing Rule of Lenity," *University of Toledo Law Review* 33 (2002): 511, 514–16.

303. Berman, *Law and Revolution*, 260–67.

304. Robert E. Rodes, *Lay Authority and Reformation in the English Church: Edward I to the Civil War* (Notre Dame: University of Notre Dame Press, 1982), 31.

305. Arthur R. Hogue, *Origins of the Common Law* 38–44 (1966; reprint, Indianapolis: Liberty Fund, 1986), 39.

306. Quoted in Hogue, *Origins of the Common Law*, 41.

307. Berman, *Law and Revolution*, 256; Hogue, *Origins of the Common Law*, 43; William Searle Holdsworth, *A History of English Law* (3rd ed., Boston: Little, Brown, 1922), 1:615. See also Carl H. Esbeck, "Dissent and Disestablishment: The Church-State Settlement in the Early American Republic," *BYU Law Review* 2004:1385, 1405–07.

308. John Calvin, *Institutes of the Christian Religion*, Henry Beveridge, trans. (Grand Rapids: Eerdmans, 1979), 4.11.7. Unless noted otherwise, future quotations from Calvin's institutes are from this translation.

309. *See* Berman, *Law and Revolution*, 267; Harold J. Berman, *Law and Revolution II* (Cambridge: Harvard University Press, 2003), 309. For the sake of historical accuracy, though, it must be noted that the story of ecclesiastical jurisdiction's restriction is quite complex. In England, the constriction of ecclesiastical jurisdiction was actually begun before the Protestant Reformation proper reached that country. The coincidence of this constriction with the Protestant Ref-

ormation was certainly mutually reinforcing. At the same time, ecclesiastical jurisdiction on a variety of issues remained important for the century following the early Reformation. See R.H. Helmholz, *Roman Canon Law in Reformation England* (Cambridge: Cambridge University Press, 1990), 28–54.

310. William Blackstone, *Commentaries on the Laws of England* (1765), 1:376. Benefit of clergy was one of the aspects of ecclesiastical jurisdiction that was abolished in the early reformation era. Helmholz, *Roman Canon Law in Reformation England*, 159; Spector, "The Sentencing Rule of Lenity," 516.

311. This in turn grew from the fact that "the reformers rejected," as a general proposition, the typical "medieval distinction between the 'sacred' and the 'secular.'" Alister E. McGrath, *Reformation Thought: An Introduction*, 3d ed. (Oxford: Blackwell Publishers, 1999), 265.

312. Calvin, *Institutes*, 4.11.15. Calvin went on to cite the example of Ambrose in detail. *Id.*

313. Ibid.

314. See generally Justo L. Gonzalez, *Essential Theological Terms* (Louisville: Westminster John Knox, 2005), 140; Alister E. McGrath, *The Christian Theology Reader* (Oxford: Blackwell, 2001), section 7.13.

315. In Luther's thought, "Ordination is a rite of the Church, but it confers no invisible grace and no indelible status. The minister is a Christian set apart by the congregation for the performance of a particular office. He is not thereby constituted a priest because Christians were priests." Roland H. Bainton, *The Reformation of the Sixteenth Century* (Boston: Beacon Press, 1952), 47. *See also* McGrath, *Reformation Thought*, 118, 203, 223.

316. *See, e.g.*, Calvin, *Institutes*, 4.11.15 (criticizing the clergy for refusing to "answer before a civil judge in personal causes").

317. Massachusetts Body of Liberties (1641), para. 59, in *Old South Leaflets* (Boston: Directors of the Old South Work), 7: 268–69, online at http://history.hanover.edu/texts/masslib.html.

318. Watson v. Jones, 80 U.S. 679, 732–33 (1872).

319. *See, e.g.*, McKelvey v. Pierce, 800 A.2d 840, 851 (N.J. 2002); Dolquist v. Heartland Presbytery, 2004 WL 74318 (D. Kan. 2004).

320. Serbian Eastern Orthodox Diocese for U. S. of America and Canada v. Milivojevich, 426 U.S. 696, 713 (1976).

321. Heroux v. Carpentier, 1998 WL 388298 (R.I. Super. Ct. 1998).

322. *Id.*, at *9.

323. *Id.*

324. *Id.* at *10.

325. "Neutral laws of general applicability" would be applied. Newport Church of Nazarene v. Hensley, 56 P.3d 386 (Or. 2002) (Title VII claim for sexual harassment not barred by autonomy considerations, because it is a neutral law of general applicability). See also Employment Division v. Smith, 494 U.S. 872 (1990) and Reynolds v. United States, 98 U.S. 145 (1879).

326. Calvin, *Institutes*, 4.11.3.

327. For an example of this, consider Martin Bucer (1538): "From this we can see the difference between the discipline and correction exercised by rulers and that exercised by carers of souls. Even when the civil authority fulfills its office of warning against and punishing wrong with the greatest diligence, it is still necessary for the church to have its own discipline and correction, which are practiced in the name of Christ and by his Holy Spirit in accordance with his command about the keys." Martin Bucer, *Concerning the True Care of Souls*, trans. Peter Beale (Edinburgh: Banner of Truth, 2009), 143. *See also* Calvin, *Institutes*, 4.11.3; Robert Linder, *The Political Ideas of Pierre Viret* (Geneva: Droz, 1964), 77, 79.

328. For others, see Marjorie A. Shields, Annotation, "Construction and Application of Church Autonomy Doctrine," 123 A.L.R. 5th 385 (2004).

329. There are some cases that seem to overstep the bounds, however. For example, a federal trial court upheld judicial cognizance of negligent supervision claims against a church. Smith v. Raleigh Dist. of North Carolina Conference of United Methodist Church, 63 F. Supp. 2d 694 (E.D. N.C. 1999). Yet, as we saw in our earlier discussion of Heroux v. Carpentier, 1998 WL 388298 (R.I. Super. Ct. 1998), the inquiry into supervisory negligence seems to implicate church polity.

330. People v. Campobello, 810 N.E.2d 307 (Ill. App. 2004).

331. Newport Church of Nazarene v. Hensley, 56 P.3d 386 (Or. 2002).

332. Under Title VII, this is called the "ministerial exception" (the same concept as church autonomy doctrine, but different terminology).

333. Bollard v. California Province of the Society of Jesus, 196 F.3d 940 (9th Cir. 1999).

334. South Jersey Catholic School teachers Organization v. St. Teresa of the Infant Jesus Church Elementary School, 696 A.2d 709 (N.J. 1997).

335. Jones v. Wolf, 443 U.S. 595, 602 (1979) (quoting Maryland & Va. Churches v. Sharpsburg Church, 396 U.S. 367, 368 (1970) (Brennan, J., concurring)).

CHAPTER 9

336.   For an example of an unsympathetic portrait of church discipline, see Alexandra Alter, "Banned from Church," *Wall Street Journal,* January 18, 2008, online at http://online.wsj.com/article/SB120061470848399079.

337.   In the following sections, we can only scratch the surface of the exegetical, theological, and pastoral issues that need to be considered in the practice of church discipline.   For an in-depth study on the theology of church discipline, see Jonathan Leeman, *The Church and the Surprising Offense of God's Love: Reintroducing the Doctrines of Church Membership and Discipline* (Wheaton: Crossway, 2010).   For a valuable work of practical pastoral advice, see Jay E. Adams, *Handbook of Church Discipline* (Grand Rapids: Zondervan, 1986).   For a plea for churches to take church discipline seriously, see Daniel Juster, *Due Process* (Shippensburg, Pennsylvania: Destiny Image, 1992).

338.   The Greek term used in this passage, "ecclesia"—translated as "church"—corresponds to the Hebrew term "kehila" or congregation, a concept Jesus' disciples would have been familiar with already.   See Juster, *Due Process*.

339.   See also John 20:23.

340.   Juster, *Due Process*, 43–44.

341.   See Juster, *Due Process*, 45–46.

342.   Fausset writes in commentary on this verse: "15. admonish him as a brother—not yet excommunicated (cf. Lev. xix. 17). Do not shun him in contemptuous silence, but tell him why he is so avoided (Matt. xviii. 15; 1 Thess. v. 14)." A. R. Fausset, in Robert Jamieson, A.R. Fausset, and David Brown, *A Commentary Critical, Experimental and Practical on the Old and New Testaments* (Grand Rapids: Eerdmans, 1961), 6:479.

343.   In a recent book, Jonathan Leeman offers one of the most thorough theological examinations of church discipline ever written—interpreting the entire process in light of what it should teach us about the love of God.   See Jonathan Leeman, *The Church and the Surprising Offense of God's Love: Reintroducing the Doctrines of Church Membership and Discipline* (Wheaton: Crossway, 2010).

344.   Martin Bucer, *Concerning the True Care of Souls*, trans. Peter Beale, (Edinburgh: Banner of Truth, 2009), 70.   For another example, consider the list offered by the Westminster Confession more than a century later, Westminster Confession XXX, 3.

345.   Quoted by R. Albert Mohler, Jr., *Church Discipline: The Missing Mark, in The Compromised Church,* John Armstrong, ed. (1998), available online at http://www.founders.org/library/polity/mohler.htm.

346. Belgic Confession, Article 30.

347. From the chapter "Order in Church and State" in John Calvin, *Truth of All Time: A Brief Outline of the Christian Faith*, trans. Stuart Olyott (Edinburgh: Banner of Truth, 2008).

CHAPTER 10

348. "Disciplinarian Procedures in the Early Church," in Everett Ferguson, ed., *Christian Life: Ethics, Morality, and Discipline in the Early Church* (New York: Garland, 1993), 272.

349. H.B. Swete, "Penitential Discipline in the First Three Centuries," *Journal of Theological Studies* 4 (1903): 321, *reprinted in* Ferguson, ed., *Christian Life*, 253.

350. *Id.*, at 257, 261–64.

351. See Amy Nelson Burnett, *The Yoke of Christ: Martin Bucer and Christian Discipline* (Kirksville: Sixteenth Century Journal Publishers, 1994), 10–11.

352. Burnett, *The Yoke of Christ*, 11–12.

353. Burnett, *The Yoke of Christ*, 13–17.

354. Auguste Boudinhon, "Ecclesiastical Discipline," in *The Catholic Encyclopedia* (New York: Robert Appleton Company, 1909) vol. 5, online at http://www.newadvent.org/cathen/05030a.htm (last visited 5 July 2012).

355. Burnett, *The Yoke of Christ*, 16–18

356. George Joyce, "Power of the Keys," in *The Catholic Encyclopedia*, vol. 8 (1910), online at http://www.newadvent.org/cathen/08631b.htm, (last visited 5 July 2012)

357. For one example, see Burnett, *The Yoke of Christ*, 92.

358. Burnett, *The Yoke of Christ*, 20–21.

359. Burnett, *The Yoke of Christ*, 21.

360. John Calvin, *Institutes of the Christian Religion*, Henry Beveridge, trans. (Grand Rapids: Eerdmans, 1979), 4.12.1.

361. The Irish Articles of Religion (1615), Section 70, include identical language.

362. Westminster Confession of Faith (1647), XXX.

363. Westminster Confession of Faith (1647), XXX.

364. London Baptist Confession (1689), ch. 26 ¶ 12. The full Confession is avail-

able online at http://www.reformed.org/documents/baptist_1689.html.

365. John Calvin, *Truth of All Time: A Brief Outline of the Christian Faith*, trans. Stuart Olyott (Edinburgh: Banner of Truth, 1998).

366. From the 1975 translation, Grand Rapids: CRC Publications.

367. *Id.*, 66–68.

368. R. Albert Mohler, Jr., "Church Discipline: The Missing Mark," in John Armstrong, ed., *The Compromised Church* (Wheaton: Crossway Books, 1998), available online at http://www.founders.org/library/polity/mohler.htm (last visited 5 July 2012).

369. James P. Boyce, "Church Discipline—Its Importance," *Southern Baptist*, February 18, 1852, reprinted in Founders Journal 73 (Summer 2008) 11, available at http://www.founders.org/journal/fj73/article1.html.

370. Boyce, "Church Discipline—Its Importance," http://www.founders.org/journal/fj73/article1.html. The Seminary that Boyce founded also issued a document, *Abstract of Principles of The Southern Baptist Theological Seminary* (1858), which lists church discipline as one of the identifying marks of a church. See Mohler, "Church Discipline: The Missing Mark," http://www.founders.org/library/polity/mohler.htm. Two of the earliest Reformed confessions explicitly articulated this position—the Belgic Confession of 1561 and the Helvetic Confession of 1566.

371. "Church Discipline in the Christian Congregation: A Report of the Commission on Theology and Church Relations, Lutheran Church—Missouri Synod," November 1985, available at http://www.iclnet.org/pub/resources/text/wittenberg/mosynod/web/cdis.html (last visited last visited 5 July 2012).

372. *Id.*

CHAPTER 11

373. For several of the following points, we are indebted to the excellent summary by H. Wayne House, "Church Discipline and the Courts," *Southern Baptist Journal of Theology* 4 (2000): 60–75. It is available online at http://www.sbts.edu/resources/journal-of-theology/sbjt-44-winter-2000/church-discipline-and-the-courts/.

374. See, e.g., Westbrook v. Penley, 231 S.W.3d 389 (Tex. 2007); Linke v. Church of Jesus Christ of Latter Day Saints, 71 Cal. App. 2d 667 (1945) ("A religious organization of this character is purely voluntary and one who joins the society 'submits himself to the disciplinary power of the body.' His rights as a mem-

ber are governed by the constitution and by-laws which he has chosen as his guide and precept, hence, the courts will not interfere unless it appears that the church authorities have proceeded contrary to the rules of the association."); Trustees of Pencader Presbyterian Church v. Gibson, 22 A.2d 782 (Del. 1941); Canovaro v. Brothers of The Order of Hermits of St. Augustine, 191 A. 140, 145 (Pa. 1937) ("it follows that their rights and obligations as members are governed by the laws of that denomination, since the voluntary act of joining the church subjects them to its rules and regulations"); Carter v. Papineau, 111 N.E. 358 (Mass. 1916); Krecker v. Shirey, 30 A. 440, 442–43 (Pa. 1894); Farnsworth v. Storrs, 59 Mass. 412, 415–16 (1850); see also House, "Church Discipline and the Courts." Compare also Order of St. Benedict v. Steinhauser, 234 U.S. 640 (1914) (discussing voluntary association with a religious order).

375. See cases cited above, at note 371.

376. See, e.g., McKelvey v. Pierce, 800 A.2d 840, 851 (N.J. 2002); Dolquist v. Heartland Presbytery, 2004 WL 74318 (D. Kan. 2004).

377. House, "Church Discipline and the Courts," 60–75.

378. For a more extensive discussion of confidentiality for pastors, see Jay E. Adams, *Handbook of Church Discipline* (Grand Rapids: Zondervan, 1986), 30–33.

379. Richard W. Garnett, "Pluralism, Dialogue, and Freedom: Professor Robert Rodes and the Church-State Nexus," *Journal of Law & Religion* 22 (2006-2007): 503, 521.

380. Chase v. Cheney, 58 Ill. 509, 535 (1871).

CHAPTER 12

381. See, e.g., Harris v. Matthews, 643 S.E.2d 566, (N.C. 2007), and Westbrook v. Penley, 231 S.W.3d 389 (Tex. 2007).

382. Richard W. Garnett, "Church, State, and the Practice of Love," *Villanova Law Review* 52 (2007): 281, 293.

383. Carl H. Esbeck, "Protestant Dissent and the Virginia Disestablishment, 1776-1786," *Georgetown Journal of Law & Public Policy* 7 (2009): 51, 103.

384. Westbrook v. Penley, 231 S.W.3d at 395.